AN
ALTERNATIVE
TO WAR OR
SURRENDER

AN ALTERNATIVE TO WAR OR SURRENDER

CHARLES E. OSGOOD

UNIVERSITY OF ILLINOIS PRESS
Urbana, Chicago, London

To my son Philip and my daughter Gail, in the hope that their
children will be born into a more secure world.

© 1962 by the Board of Trustees of the University of Illinois
Manufactured in the United States of America
Library of Congress Catalog Card No. 62-19089
Second printing, 1970

252   72312   0

PREFACE TO THIS EDITION

In lecturing about the strategy of graduated and reciprocated initiatives in tension-reduction (GRIT for short) as a means of resolving conflicts between nations before audiences of many kinds and in many places over the past ten years, the question that most often comes up in discussion is this: what impact have you had upon people in power? Is anyone up there listening? This is a very difficult question to answer. If anyone up there *were* listening, he would not be likely to attribute his actions to a psychologist (popularly conceived of as a "head-shrinker"). And since there have been many voices other than mine speaking for similar strategies of de-escalation, one would be hard put to identify his own as the influential one.

Nevertheless, there have been encouraging signs. There was what Amitai Etzioni has referred to as "The Kennedy Experiment" (*The Western Political Science Quarterly*, 1967, *20,* 361-380), a pattern of initiatives begun by the late president in his American University speech on June 10, 1963, interwoven with reciprocations by the Soviet Union, clearly accompanied by relaxation of mutual tensions, and only ended by Kennedy's assassination on November 22, 1963.

More recently there have been the gross initiative by President Johnson of pulling back the bombing of North Vietnam, the graduated troop withdrawals of the Nixon administration and, as I write, Nixon's gesture to remove trade barriers from "goods made in Communist China." And, oh yes, *Esquire Magazine* has included GRIT as one of its ten Peace Plans in a recent issue! Perhaps the most encouraging thing is that when one moves around Washington now, as compared to ten years ago, the strategy of calculated deescalation of tensions is no longer being talked about as a radical and rather dangerous business, but rather is accepted as a quite ordinary alternative. Anonymity is a very small price to pay for banality in a case like this.

How has this alternative achieved familiarity in the short space of a decade? In some part it has been the result of much lecturing and writing of paperback books by many academic types like myself. In some part it has been the explosion of research on conflict resolution in the scientific community — "peace research" is no longer a dirty word. But in much larger part, I think, it has been due to the continuing pressure being applied by concerned and enlightened citizens to their representatives in government. I have been deeply gratified by the numbers of letters I have received from people in all walks of life expressing support for my ideas and indicating that they have forwarded these ideas to people "up there." Just last year a young woman in a small midwestern college wrote me that *An Alternative to War or Surrender* had been used as a text in a large class, and the class had voted to send their marked-up copies to every senator in Washington.

GRIT does not have the glamour of Overkill or Safeguard as a strategic alternative. It continues to need representation, again and again, to the government by the people. It is, therefore, with gratification and hope that I write this little preface.

Charles E. Osgood
Urbana, Illinois
December 25, 1969

CONTENTS

THE FUTURE OF MAN

1

The future of man is always in the process of becoming. The number of possible futures is almost infinite, but some are much more likely than others. Forces arising in the deep past point mute fingers toward some paths but not toward others. The actions we take today—both as individuals and as nations—are like wagers put on one course as against another. Only by exercising our uniquely human capacity to look ahead and plan can we affect our own future. And then, we can influence it only by what we do today.

Let us lift aside the veil of tomorrow and look quickly at a few of the many possible futures for man.

ONE FUTURE: A WORLD COMMUNAL

Outwardly, the United States is at peace. There are few soldiers on the streets. Loudspeakers at every city street corner and in every village square alternate praise for the system and exhortation to greater communal effort, interspersed with bits of inspiring music. But it is the same everywhere, and monotonous. The people go about the necessary business of doing what they must to stay alive—working in the factory or the field, attending the regular meetings of their commune, repeating on demand the new sacred phrases. But they are a drab and shoddy people. They dress much alike, eat much alike, and apparently think much alike. Things are much the same the world over.

But beneath this passive surface all is not peaceful. Although no one dares to express himself too freely, except to old and close friends, everyone thinks his private thoughts. Resistance to the system comes out in subtle ways that are difficult to prevent: innovation in science and industry has practically ceased; production has been steadily falling, despite the constant exhortations and even some more violent measures; newspapers are looked at but not read; the birth rate has gone down sharply. True, this resistance is greatest in mature adults, those who grew up in the more colorful world of yesterday. Young adults display a different reaction to the system: they are violent and unpredictable, a constant thorn in the side of authority. Only in the communal schools, where the noble experiment of democracy is at best a vague and distorted memory, does the youngest generation bear the promise of a glowing Communist future.

How did the world get this way? Back somewhere along the path a basic choice was made: to depend almost exclusively on nuclear weapons for the defense of our way of life. The trouble was that these weapons were always too terrible to use—particularly when the other side had equally terrible ones—and the issue of the moment never quite justified the means. So nations around the world, faced with their own internal problems and given little help with them by the United States, fell away from the Free World one by one. Finally, isolated in an alien world and torn internally by militant rightists and militant leftists alike, the government of the United States fell apart, and in the confusion a kind of communism took over. Gradually this way of life will evolve and change through its own internal dynamics, but how many generations, how many centuries, will it take?

ANOTHER FUTURE: PAX AMERICANA

Outwardly, the world is at peace. No nation—but one—has armaments, nuclear or otherwise. Within nations, no group—but one—has even hand weapons. Yet nowhere do people seem to be as happy and secure as they ought to be in a world at peace. Soldiers dressed in olive drab and armed with fantastic nuclear hand weapons are to be seen everywhere, but always in tight, wary groups. The local people eye them with distaste, insult them with innuendo, and even attack them with abandon when any opportunity is given. These are American soldiers and they are maintaining the peace. But one has only to look closely into the faces of the men in olive drab to realize that they do not enjoy maintaining this peace.

Inwardly, the United States is at war. It is ruled by military dictatorship. Soldiers outnumber civilians on the streets. Since mercenaries of other countries cannot be trusted, Americans must spread themselves thinly over the world for their own protection. Less than 5 per cent of the world's population is controlling all the rest. Highly automatized factories, run mainly by computers, turn out the devices with which Pax Americana is preserved: inspection satellites to warn of potential disturbance to the peace, weapons satellites to quell such disturbance promptly, nuclear rifles for the men in olive drab, and Geiger counters for their packs. The women work in the factories and the fields; they dress much alike (shoddily), eat much alike (poorly), and think much alike (grimly). The schools are also factories, turning out soldiers and technicians rather than scientists and scholars.

How did the world get *this* way? Back along the path the same choice to defend our way of life with weapons was made. But farther along the path, as weapons on both sides became more fantastic and as more countries fell into the Communist camp, another basic choice was made: to gamble on the advantage of surprise attack. It was believed that this would eliminate the source of military danger and what was thought to be the source of World Communism, once and for all. From a strictly military point of view, given the development of antimissile missiles, the

choice was a wise one: most of what was European Russia became an unlivable wasteland, whereas comparatively few areas
of devastation marked the United States. But what about the
human point of view? This act had clearly labeled the United
States as the aggressor, the source of threat, and therefore the
prime target for counteraggression. Always anticipating reprisal
from some quarter, we now had no choice but to police a hostile
world. For how long could this role be maintained?

AND ANOTHER FUTURE: STASIS

Under the threat of nuclear weapons and the impetus of the
cold war, the world is divided into two armed camps of roughly
equal power. There are no longer any neutrals, nor even any un-
committed countries; India was driven into the Western camp
by aggressive pressures from China, while all of Southeast Asia
was swept into the Eastern camp by internal pressures and subversion. By now the walls that began in Berlin have made a fine
but decisive cut across most of the globe. As communication and
travel across this far-flung boundary decreased, mutual distrust
and tension increased.

But the arms race has been continuing steadily, to the point
where 100-megaton bombs are commonplace. Delivery systems
have become well-nigh impregnable, either as deeply hardened
launching pads on land or as elusive nuclear-powered submarines at sea. So neither side dares to disturb the balance deliberately. Yet faced with the possibilities of accident or irrationality, and realizing what full-scale nuclear war would now mean,
civilian populations in the heartlands of the two polar powers
have been burrowing themselves deeper and deeper into the
ground. The deeper they dig, the larger the bombs are made,
and so the deeper they dig again. Great cities have become hol-
low shells; the millions of gaily colored automobiles that used to
jostle their way along countless highways are now junked and
forgotten—warning times being so short that adequate shelters
could not be reached from the surface. Television phantasies
have almost completely replaced real-life surface adventure, and
many people never leave their underground sets at all.

The ultimate in "stabilized deterrence" seems to have been
achieved in this future. But it is never stable enough. Knowing
that The Enemy (now almost a myth) will always be striving for

some advantage, each side keeps devising newer and ever more incredible means of offense and defense. Would a world that chose this course go whirling on into eternity, forever frozen in this posture of mutual deterrence? Is a species that was about to reach the stars destined to retreat back into the caves? Or will some combination of human and technical failure eventually bring this world tumbling into the very holocaust it is trying to avoid?

IF I WERE PRESIDENT

What would you do if you were President? I was once asked this question by a famous physicist, asked it on the very first moment of meeting him for the first time. I was completely at a loss, fumbled through a few idiotic suggestions, and made it perfectly obvious that the White House could well do without my services. I remember thinking at the time that it is much easier to make momentous decisions when you do not carry the load of responsibility. Nevertheless, decisions must be made. None of the futures we have sampled so far is acceptable for human beings. None of them offers the kind of world in which we would want our children to grow up. What would I do if I were President? Without meaning to be presumptuous, and realizing that the President has undoubtedly pondered over this most crucial problem of our time more deeply than anyone else, if I were in his position I would probably be thinking thoughts like these:

Total war in this nuclear age has become inconceivable, even though many about me are busily conceiving of it and planning for it. With nuclear retaliation now a certainty, military "victory" in the traditional sense has become impossible; not only would many millions of the people I am sworn to protect lose their lives, but the way of life I am sworn to preserve would be abruptly terminated. Yet we cannot surrender to the Communist way of life; that future is unacceptable. By engaging in a nuclear arms race, we have been able to deter the Communists from attacking us directly so far. But it is becoming clearer and clearer that this future is a blind alley: at best it leads to a permanently divided world based on mutual fear, with our people huddled in caves; at worst it explodes at some point into an incredible holocaust.

What, then, can be done? Can we gamble on losing less in the long run by an all-out surprise attack now? No, for not only would this fail to eliminate Communism (indeed, it would probably strengthen it), but it would isolate us in a hostile world. Is there anything we can do other than hang on grimly and hope? We can try even harder to achieve agreements with the Soviets to disarm, although so far it has proven impossible to obtain significant agreements when mutual distrust is so high.

But wait. Here—in the question of mutual distrust—may lie the key we are looking for. Would it be possible for this country to take the initiative in reducing distrust? Could we transform the spiral of fear into a spiral of hope? We would have to move very carefully and gradually, but by taking consistent tension-reducing steps, we might be able to create an atmosphere of mutual trust. Then really significant agreements on disarmament could be achieved. We would be using our immense military power not only as a deterrent but also as a base of security from which to take the initiative. Would the Russians cooperate in this effort as it became clear what we were attempting? I think they might —for reasons of good sense even if not for reasons of good will— and, in any case, we could test them without seriously jeopardizing our own security. This approach would not be easy or simple in the world as it exists today; it would be extraordinarily difficult and complicated, but it could lead us gradually in a direction we want to go.

Having reached this point in my thinking (if I were President), I would give this policy an appropriate technical name—*Graduated Reciprocation in Tension-reduction* (whose initials, happily, form the word GRIT, which is both easily remembered and full of persistence). Then I would set my experts to work giving it a thorough evaluation for feasibility. If they decided it could be done within reasonable limits of security, even though admittedly difficult and complicated, I would then choose the right moment and introduce it. Certainly this approach would be a gamble, but it would point toward a more acceptable future, one in which we could both preserve our lives *and* our way of life.

DO UNTO OTHERS. . . .

Another future.

"My friends and countrymen. Tonight I speak not only to you, but also to the peoples of the entire world and their leaders. For in truth we are already one world, whether we desire it so or not, and the fate of each of us is bound up with that of his brother. Whether it be war or peace, all people and all nations are involved; none can escape the ravages of the first or the blessings of the second. Therefore I ask you to study carefully what I say tonight.

"In the past two decades, man's scientific genius has changed just about everything in our world—except human nature. Today I could be talking by telephone with Prime Minister Nehru in India within a few minutes; it takes less time to travel from Washington to Moscow today than it took our forefathers to travel from Boston to Providence; indeed, tomorrow we shall be straining for the stars.

"Today the United States stands poised with incredible military power; our capacity for destruction is many hundred times that possessed by all nations during World War II. The Soviet Union has similar capacity for destruction. Were all this terrible power to be released in war, it is doubtful if civilization as we cherish it would survive.

"The leaders of all nations know this is true. They also know that there is no defense against nuclear weapons, except fear of their use. I know this. Premier Khrushchev knows this. Yet we keep preparing for the war that no one wants to fight. We keep moving through crisis after crisis, each more threatening than the last. Is man incapable of controlling the power his genius has created? Are there no alternatives to war or the surrender of one side to the other?

"Premier Khrushchev has repeatedly stated that Communism is willing to compete for men's hearts and minds by means other than war, in what he calls 'peaceful coexistence.' The Free World accepts this challenge. It is a battle we have hardly begun to fight, and I am confident that steadily and certainly we will win it.

"But how are we first to win and then keep the peace? Both the United States and the Soviet Union have offered proposals for general and complete disarmament, with guarantees of adequate inspection as bases for negotiation. But despite agreement on our expressed goals, prolonged negotiations have only resulted in haggling over details, with no real progress, while crisis has followed crisis and tensions have steadily mounted. We must continue to strive, even harder and with full sincerity, to reach agreements on disarmament. But this is not enough. We must begin *now* to create an atmosphere of mutual trust in which successful negotiations will become more possible. We must begin *now* to reduce and then control international tensions.

"How can this be done, in a world torn by strife and smothered by distrust? It can be done by putting the arms race in reverse. The arms race is a tension-inducing system in which each side, acting on its own initiative, takes small but repeated steps to increase its military strength, each step threatening the other into taking armament steps of its own. In a nuclear age, the arms race is leading the human race into a desperate blind alley. But it is possible to walk back out of this situation in much the same way we walked into it. Each nation can, acting on its own initiative and operating within reasonable limits of security, take small but repeated steps designed to reduce tensions; if the opponent also desires to avoid the grim consequences of nuclear war, he can respond with tension-reducing initiatives of his own. Thus, together, they can reach safer and saner grounds for their dispute.

"I challenge all nations, including those in the Communist bloc, to join us in a march toward peace. From time to time the United States will initiate steps designed to reduce world tensions. I will announce these steps prior to their execution, and on the dates set *these steps will be taken.* Individually, they may seem of small significance, but they will be cumulative, and they will increase in significance if and as they are matched by actions of other nations. I promise you that our actions will have the sincere purpose of reducing tensions. I ask the leaders of all nations to support this effort, and particularly I invite the leadership of the Communist bloc to join us in this march toward a more peaceful world. If they are sincere in their expressed desire for general and complete disarmament, they will be willing to take small but steady steps toward that goal. Together we can move, step by careful step, back away from the abyss that threatens to engulf us all.

"And now I announce to the world our first steps in the march toward peace. As of February 1, I have asked our space agency to make public all medical information we have been gathering concerning man-in-space; I invite all other nations to reciprocate in kind. On that same day, all discriminatory trade and travel restrictions with respect to the Chinese People's Republic will be lifted and we will entertain diplomatic exchange; I invite the leaders of this great nation to reciprocate in kind. On March 1, all American military forces in two overseas bases, one in Turkey and one in Japan, will be withdrawn, the bases will be deactivated, and we will begin constructing international universities on their sites; we invite both United Nations and Communist teams of inspectors to observe these actions and verify their execution; we invite all nations to join with us in the building and staffing of these new international universities.

"In conclusion, I want to make one thing perfectly clear—to our friends, to our present enemies, and to our own people. The United States is taking these steps toward the control of world tensions of its own free will, on its own initiative, and because of its desire for peace. We are not acting under any duress or any outside pressure. We retain our capacity to wreak intolerable nuclear devastation upon any nation that would dare to attack us, and we intend to stand firm and resist any attempt to take advantage of our good will. But it is our sincere purpose to use this tremendous power for peace rather than for war, as a source of security rather than merely as a source of fear. Again, I challenge all nations to join us in a calculated, self-controlled march toward a more peaceful world."

EXCERPTS FROM LEASED WIRE NEWS REPORTS

JAN. 15:   No matter what agency of government, Pentagon or State Department, no matter which side of Congress you ask, reaction to the President's "March Toward Peace" speech last night is split right down the middle. Senator Stone said flatly, "This means surrender to Communism," and Congressman Steele, Chairman of the Armed Services Committee, stated that our armed forces must be put on double alert to repel the attack which will certainly come. But Senator Amsdell of the Foreign Relations Committee had this to say: "For the first time in many years the United States has seized the initiative in foreign policy; we are probing the Soviet's willingness to work for peace without weakening our own position. We must stand behind our President in this courageous effort." Reaction from allied and neutral countries is almost uniformly favorable. Great Britain has already announced it will also make public its scientific knowledge on man-in-space on February 1, and it urges Russia to cooperate. Prime Minister Nehru said the President has brought new hope to an anxious world. But the Communist bloc has greeted the President's speech with absolute silence—with the exception of Marshal Tito of Yugoslavia, who stated that the sincerity of the United States will be tested by what it does, not by what it says.

FEB. 1: The United States, Great Britain, and several other countries today made public scientific information of a medical nature on man-in-space. No action has been taken by the Soviet Union, and *Pravda* reasserted its view that this is a "Capitalist trick." A large number of newspapermen and scientists have been granted permission by the State Department to travel in Red China, but the Chinese government has refused their admission. Despite Mao's statement of last week—that "the world is seeing the death throes of the Paper Tiger"—there is already a boom on trade in Chinese goods from the mainland.

FEB. 15: Today the President announced that, as of April 1, the right of Soviet and Chinese diplomats, trade representatives, and tourists to travel in the United States with minimal restriction will be extended; he invited reciprocation in kind. He also announced that, as of the same date, this country will make available to the UN technicians and professionals for work in the Congo and other areas; he invited cooperation in this program from all highly industrialized countries. The President restated the nature of his "March Toward Peace" policy. There has been no change in the Communist position. This morning the delegation of neutralist nations, headed by India's Nehru, arrived in Moscow for talks with Premier Khrushchev; it is understood that they will urge Soviet participation in the "March Toward Peace." The delegation flies to New York next week.

FEB. 20: The Birch Society today called for impeachment of the President of the United States, for deliberately trying to bring about surrender of his country to Communism, and it demanded that Congress take action immediately. The President was unavailable for comment, but his press secretary made public a prepared statement. "We are engaged in a great experiment for peace," said the President. "We are strong and determined. We retain the military power to annihilate completely any nation or combination of nations that tries to take advantage of our good will. We will steadfastly continue to apply pressure on our opponents to join the March Toward Peace, until it becomes perfectly clear from their inaction that they prefer war to peace."

MARCH 1: Observers from both the United Nations and the Soviet Union today inspected the two bases in Turkey and Japan and verified the fact that American forces had been withdrawn and the bases deactivated. On the Senate floor, Senator Stone demanded impeachment of the President. The Vice-President ruled that the impeachment motion would be opened for debate after present business on the docket was concluded. A straw ballot of Congress conducted by this news service indicates a split, largely on party lines, and insufficient votes for the necessary two thirds for impeachment. General Jones of the Joint Chiefs of Staff stated in a speech yesterday that the President is the Commander-in-Chief of all U.S. military forces, and as long as he is in power must make the final decisions; however, he warned that although we are still the most powerful nation on earth, continued "giveaways" will destroy our security.

APRIL 12: Premier Khrushchev today made an important announcement. He stated that the Union of Soviet Socialist Republics was dedicated to peace. Khrushchev said that, as of June 1, all Russian and East German military personnel and weapons would be withdrawn from Berlin, leaving only ordinary police; he invited inspection by our authorities and requested reciprocation in kind. The Russian leader stated that if this step were matched, on September 1 Russian forces in East Germany would be reduced by half; equivalent reductions would be expected from the West, he said.

APRIL 15: Today Senator Stone's motion for impeachment of the President was resoundingly defeated, by a vote of 78 to 22. Immediately the President thanked Congress for its support and promised to continue working for peace with security. Meanwhile, entirely without fanfare, the Soviet Union today released a 4,000-page document in Russian, English, French, and Chinese detailing medical information on man-in-space. Nehru's flying neutralist team arrived in Peking this morning; they were greeted with a mammoth demonstration of flag-waving civilians and marching soldiers. Mao demanded that the Soviet Union stand firm against the blandishments of the "Paper Tiger."

JUNE 1: An Allied inspection team today verified the removal of Soviet and East German military personnel from East Berlin. The President announced that, by agreements previously arrived at with Great Britain and France, Allied military personnel were already moving from West Berlin, and he invited reciprocal Soviet inspection. The President also announced today that at the next convening of the General Assembly of the UN on September 20, our delegation would move the seating of Red China; he requested that Communist China reciprocate by formally acknowledging the existence and independence of Taiwan as a separate state; he reasserted the willingness of the United States to entertain diplomatic exchange with China and requested removal of their restrictions on travel by U.S. nationals. The Soviet Union has still made no comment on providing technicians for the Congo and other "have-not" countries under UN auspices. However, a Soviet trade commission arrived today in New York.

AUG. 10:   Chancellor Adenauer today complained bitterly that the United States, with the assistance of France and Great Britain, was "sacrificing all hopes for a strong and unified Germany on the altar of appeasement to Communism." Meanwhile, in Washington, Congressman Steele demanded an investigation of the Arms Control and Disarmament Agency to determine if it was secretly plotting surrender of our country to Communism by appeasement and disarmament; the Congressman hinted that known Communists and fellow travelers were in high places in the Agency. But from the White House came announcement of two more steps in the President's "March Toward Peace." On September 15 our remaining bases in Japan will be publicly denuclearized; UN, Russian, and Chinese observers have been invited to inspect and verify this action; reciprocation is invited, but left open-ended as to form. On September 1, in response to Soviet initiatives, West Germany will be denuclearized, under public observation, but NATO conventional forces will not be reduced at this time.

SEPT. 16:   Bulletin! Red China has stepped up bombardment of the islands of Quemoy and Matsu. Invasion preparations have been observed. U.S. naval power is already concentrated near these islands, and the President has just issued firm warnings that any encroachment on the islands will be repulsed by force. Khrushchev has warned that use of nuclear weapons by the U.S. on China will be answered by nuclear attack on the U.S. Senator Stone has called for nuclear force to eliminate the threat of Communist China once and for all; Senator Amsdell has asked for firm calmness from our government leaders, our mass media, and our people.

SEPT. 18:   A predawn invasion attempt by Mao's forces on Quemoy and Matsu was decisively repulsed by the American Navy. Only conventional weapons were employed by both sides. Under Presidential order, U.S. action was pinpointed to repulsing the invasion attempt; no counterattack on the Chinese mainland has occurred or is planned. General Jones announced to the press that our failure to follow up with a nuclear bombardment of the mainland would encourage the Chinese to attack Formosa by air. Chiang Kai-shek's military forces have not been employed in this action so far, but remain on 24-hour alert. It is reported that high-level Russo-Chinese policy talks are under way.

SEPT. 20:   Amidst mass demonstrations around the UN building organized by the Birch Society and the Committee of a Million, the chief delegate of the United States to this international body today moved the seating of Red China in the General Assembly, thereby fulfilling the promise of a previous announcement. Congress is up in arms. From the White House, the President stated that the situation in Quemoy and Matsu is fully under control, although the bombardment is continuing, and that the "March Toward Peace" will continue. The Chinese must learn, he said, that our "March Toward Peace," while sincere, does not mean surrender. He also announced two more steps. First, beginning with the college year in September of next year, student exchanges will be offered in proportion to the populations of the countries involved; this means that relatively large numbers of Chinese students will be welcomed, if they apply; he requested reciprocation in spirit. Second, as of January 1, our DEW-line (early warning system) will be made bidirectional (warning of any attack by us on Russia as well as vice versa); the Soviets are invited to "plug in" as of that date. The President stated that this emphasizes our determination not to attack by surprise with intercontinental nuclear missiles.

SEPT. 25:   Today a delegation from Red China arrived at the UN and presented its credentials. The bombardment of Quemoy and Matsu, in the process of petering out for the past few days, ceased this morning. Mao has not made any statement about the status of Taiwan, however. Meanwhile, Premier Khrushchev has asserted the solidarity of the Socialist Peoples' Governments, the friendship of the Soviet Union for China, and has indicated that the Soviet delegation in the UN will move for the substitution of Communist China for Nationalist China on the Security Council. Khrushchev also invited U.S. space scientists to cooperate with Soviet space scientists, under UN auspices, in an attempt to land two men—one Russian, the other American—on the surface of the moon. "Mighty Soviet boosters will lift them from the earth," he said, "and sensitive American guidance systems will get them there." He set January 1 as the date to begin this joint effort.

NOV. 1:   Today, while a U.S. diplomatic mission held secret talks with Mao in Vienna, and while the Russian and American delegations at the UN joined in moving the substitution of Communist China for Nationalist China on the Security Council, the President announced a greatly expanded economic aid program for Taiwan. Newsmen on this island report agitation from the Taiwanese for increased representation in Chiang's government. This morning the

New York Times announced that, beginning on December 1, its Sunday editions would include a section on international issues prepared by Soviet and other foreign sources, clearly labeled as such but without censorship; it said that it had requested reciprocation from *Izvestia* and other important foreign newspapers. "It is a good thing to know what other people are thinking," the *Times* editorial said. The Soviet Union announced that it was opening itself to completely unrestricted travel by other nationals, with the sole exception of certain specified military installations. Under strong urging from the British Commonwealth and India, plans for full-scale disarmament negotiations under UN auspices are being planned for next spring. The President left this morning for a month of relaxation in his vacation White House; smiling, he promised newsmen to keep in touch.

Another possible future—does it seem utterly fantastic? I have no crystal ball, of course, and it certainly would not work out exactly this way. There would be more complications, more harried communications back and forth, more misunderstandings and clarifications. Yet it is one of many possible futures, and certainly much more acceptable than the others we have sampled. Which is the most likely future for man? It depends on people. The future is always in the process of becoming, and the likelihood of one as against another depends upon what we do today.

CULTURE LAG

Today we stand in a deadly dilemma—between weapons against which there is no defense and international tensions from which there seems to be no relief. We have almost arrived at that point in human history when the two major nuclear powers will be able to wipe each other off the face of the earth in almost less time than it will take you to read this little book. This grim view of the situation is acknowledged by almost everyone who has written about policy in the nuclear age.

Our situation is completely novel to human experience, and it will certainly require a novel solution if we are to end up *neither* Red nor Dead. Yet despite the novelty of the problem, relations among nations today are still being conducted along traditional lines, and being habitual these traditional policies are felt to be "realistic." Leaders on both sides keep talking about achieving peace and security through ever-increasing military power, when our reason as well as our experience tell us that the peace thus attained is ephemeral and the security an illusion.

The truth of the matter is that we are caught in a great cultural lag. Our facility in technology has completely outstripped our ability to understand and control ourselves. This generation is faced with the consequences of the imbalance between our skill in the physical sciences and our ineptness in the sciences of man. Recent developments in the technology of communications and transportation—to say nothing of weaponry—have not merely made some form of world government feasible, they have made it essential if our kind of civilization is to survive.

But the problem is this: how can we get from here to there? How can we overcome this lag between our technology and our form of political organization? How can we halt, and then put into reverse, the tensions/arms race spiral in which we are caught? Only by doing this can we hope to create an atmosphere in which steps toward one world under common rule of law could be taken.

This is a little book, but at least it has a big purpose: to show that there is a way out, a way of halting and reversing the spiral of terror. It is possible for this nation to take the initiative in a strategy that would allow us to march deliberately toward a more peaceful world, yet always moving within acceptable limits of dignity and security. We can use our capacity for nuclear devastation not merely to deter through fear but also to support positive actions—actions designed ultimately to eliminate the threat of nuclear war itself.

The future is ours for the making.

THE NEANDERTHAL MENTALITY

2

Neanderthal Man was a good cut above the great apes. True, he was squat and bandy-legged, with protruding jaws, beetling brows, and a receding forehead, but he stood upright, swung a mean stone ax, and had discovered fire. For protection against a threatening environment, he lived in caves. We know almost nothing about his mentality—the bones and stones uncovered by burrowing archeologists bear only the faintest traces of his mind—but it seems likely that his primitive thoughts dealt mostly with such earthy matters as food and sex, while his most characteristic emotions were probably fear and hate.

It is generally believed that Neanderthal Man simply died out, to be replaced by Homo Sapiens. But it is at least possible that he was absorbed into the flowing tide of humanity. Perhaps Modern Man, with his head in the sky, still has Neanderthal feet that are stuck in the mire. In any case, there is much about the behavior of Homo Sapiens under stress that reflects his more primitive origins.

SOME PARADOXES OF THE NUCLEAR AGE

There are many paradoxes about the nuclear age in which we live. Recognizing them is an important first step on the road to resolving them. The Neanderthal had little patience with paradoxes, puzzles, and games. If he recognized them at all, he either bulled his way through or promptly forgot. Homo Sapiens, on the other hand, has always been intrigued by such logical problems; in fact, paradoxes have often been the steppingstones to his highest achievements in philosophy and science. Here are a few of the paradoxes of the world today.

Paradox I. The greater the destructive capacity of the weapons in our hands, the less most people seem to worry about it. I have heard it estimated by a physicist friend of mine that if all the destructive energy in nuclear weapons now stockpiled were to be transformed into its measuring unit—that is, each 10-megaton bomb transformed into 10 million tons of TNT and so forth—and if then it were to be spread evenly over the surface area of our country, we would all be wading around nearly up to our ankles in dynamite! Be that as it may, it is certainly true that never before in human history have so few been able to destroy so many and so much in so little time. Yet how many people are as worried about this as they are about the next raise or about what the fellow next door thinks of them? How many intellectuals have fully committed themselves to working on this problem, which surely by all odds is the most significant of all times? How much effort have our mass media given to the search for fresh alternatives to war? Let one madman loose on the streets of our town, and we form citizens' posses; but let hundreds of millions of tons of destruction hang over our heads, and we couldn't be less concerned, apparently.

Paradox II. While feverishly engaged in a nuclear arms race, both sides express peaceful intentions and fervent hopes that these weapons will never be used. I believe that these hopes and intentions are sincere, on both sides. Nobody wants a nuclear war. Yet roughly half the national budgets of the two polar powers go into military preparations—that is, into producing things no one expects ever to use. The Russians resume testing, and we condemn them for polluting the air with radioactive fallout. And then, with almost the same breath, we claim we must also resume testing in the atmosphere, to keep ahead in the arms race and thereby defend ourselves. Surely future generations will look back upon these grim years as the Age of Unreason.

Paradox III. The more nations spend for what they call "defense," the less real security their people have. Who will deny that over the past ten years we have been steadily increasing our expenditures for weapons? And who will deny that now we are really less safe, less secure, less defended than ever before in our national history? The reason for this is to be found in a basic fact about military technology in a nuclear age. This is the fact that offensive capability has completely outstripped defensive capability. Policy-makers are fond of talking about great defensive "shields" or "umbrellas," but these defenses are more in men's minds than their weapons. Defense in this nuclear age adds up to little more than mutual fear.

Paradox IV. The greater a nation's military power, the less seems to be its freedom of initiative in foreign policy. Witness the squashing of the Suez situation, the attempts on all sides to neutralize Laos, the Soviet backdown in the Congo, or the ambivalence of the mighty American elephant in dealing with the little Cuban mouse. Quite apart from fears of retaliation, the mere possession of nuclear weapons has a sobering, restraining effect. For rational men, at least, possession of power brings along with it a sense of responsibility. And so we find this nuclear age characterized by a Great Freeze on initiative in foreign policy.

Now if a psychologist or psychiatrist were faced with an individual human being so full of unrecognized, irrational paradoxes in his thinking, he would probably recommend that the man be institutionalized. Unfortunately there are no institutions for nations. There are not even any therapists to whom nations can go;

it all must come from within. However, the psychologist or psychiatrist would also realize that this individual's behavior only seems paradoxical because the dynamics of his case are not fully understood. In this chapter we will be looking for some of the psychological sources of such paradoxical thinking.

But, you may object, are we not dealing with the behavior of nations, not individuals? And if so, of what possible value is a psychological analysis? I would say, first, that the problems we face today *are* primarily matters of human nature and human relationships; there is nothing about nuclear science that automatically produces hydrogen bombs and nothing about space science that naturally produces missiles. It takes human decisions based upon human fears and hates to debase science this way. Second, I would argue that in the absence of any real science of international relations, what little we do know about the psychology of individual behavior may provide us with at least a model and perhaps a few good leads for understanding the behavior of nations. Furthermore, the extraordinary development of the mass media during this century has probably done much to bridge the gap between everyday people and so-called experts. The first thing the man in a Washington office does is to look through his *Times* or his *Post,* and what he sees there is not too different from what you and I read in our local newspaper.

HUMAN THINKING UNDER STRESS

When they think about it at all, I am sure most Americans and most Russians as well are aware of the dangers in our present course. Yet they feel impelled along it with a certain sense of inevitability. "We must learn to live with it," our newspapers tell us; editorials complain about the high cost of defense, but then conclude that "we must grin and pay it." What gives us this sense of inevitability? What forces us to believe that our only choice is between war or surrender? What is there about human thinking under stress that pushes every group conflict toward mutual annihilation? Let us look into the dynamics of our own minds, because only through understanding ourselves can we ever hope to understand others. Only by recognizing the Neanderthal within us can we hope to control him.

Denial

When faced with an overwhelming threat, but having no immediate way of dealing with it, the typical Neanderthal reaction is to deny its existence. Rather than holding the danger in mind and continually trying to find an acceptable solution, we simply repress it and go about doing things "as usual." To keep our minds at ease and escape unpleasant twinges of anxiety, the Neanderthal within us avoids exposure to information that might revive awareness of the danger and seeks out information that seems to promise security, no matter how illusory. In the past we rubbed a magic amulet when the saber-toothed tiger moaned; now we build a token fallout shelter and pay out bigger taxes for defense—when the Russian Bear growls.

Once conscious acceptance of the danger has been repressed, the unconscious anxiety (which is still there inside us) is free to produce what psychiatrists call *symptoms*. A typical symptom is what Edgar Allan Poe so aptly called "the imp of the perverse." This is the irrational compulsion to flirt with the threatening situation: to play with fire, to lean far out over the edge of the cliff, to play that dangerous game of "chicken" on the highways. In the nuclear world, this compulsion shows up in the urge to play "chicken" in crisis situations like Berlin or to press that critical button and get it all over with. The more one denies a danger intellectually, the less the restraint on the compulsion to flirt with it. Only people who have completely denied the dangers of nuclear war could say, "Let's go over there and bomb the hell out of them!"

The best way out of the denial dilemma is to keep the danger in mind and keep working on the problem until some acceptable solution is discovered. Then legitimate fear can be channeled into constructive action—action designed to eliminate the threat. The trouble with most pacifist approaches has been that they frighten the living daylights out of people with threats of nuclear fire and brimstone without providing any acceptable solution— acceptable, that is, within present conditions of competing sovereign states.

Remoteness

Most of the words we use to talk about nuclear war are abstract terms that get their meanings indirectly by association with other words, not directly from association with real objects and events. Words like "intercontinental missiles," "megatons," and "60 million casualties" simply do not have the emotional, gut meanings of words like "blood," "bread," and "mother." Furthermore, one cannot directly sense the danger of nuclear missiles 5,000 miles away as one can the danger in a man seen holding a club or knife. We require special gadgets to tell us that we are being exposed to lethal doses of radiation. And it takes a truly incredible feat of creative imagination to comprehend the real meaning of "60 million casualties."

The Neanderthal mentality is not particularly noted for creative imagination. It fully appreciates the danger of a swirling black funnel cloud, but has trouble with the weather report that announces its likelihood. It would fully appreciate the blast and fire storm of a nuclear explosion nearby, but would have trouble keeping in mind the equal danger of unseen radiation. This kind of mentality is prone to oversimplify the real world; it likes to think of international relations in terms of battling giants, and it answers the pacifist once and for all with the query, "What would you do if a thug tried to enter your house and murder your wife?" Seated in the backyard on a nice spring day, drinking a can of beer, watching the kids at play, and enjoying the trees and flowers, the Neanderthal within us simply cannot conceive of the trees blackened, the flowers suddenly withered, and the voices of the children stilled—or there being no more beer.

I am told that most Russians seem more deeply afraid of the dangers of a "hot" nuclear war than most Americans. Perhaps this is because well within the memories of living adults they lost nearly 20 million people under conditions of ordinary war. To make the dangers of nuclear war immediate and believable to people who have never experienced even ordinary bombing of civilians is a difficult task. It is an awful thing to say, but perhaps the best thing that could happen to us would be an accidental explosion of a nuclear warhead near some large city—with full television coverage.

Projection

"Man is the measure of all things." Surely this must be a Neanderthal epigram. The whole history of the development of human science traces a progressive freeing of his measurements from the arbitrary platform of his own senses and opinions. Copernicus removed our planet from the center of the universe; Darwin removed our species from the center of God's creative intentions; Freud removed our reason from the center of control over our behavior. But who is going to remove man's *ethnocentrism* from control over his social judgments of what is good and bad?

What a person thinks is "normal" or "natural" usually depends upon his own range of experience. What is "big" for the child may be "little" for the adult; what is obviously "risqué" to a New England grandmother is obviously "stylish" to her teen-age granddaughter. For my teen-age son to wear his trousers barely above the buttocks is obviously "sloppy"; and for Khrushchev to pound his desk at the United Nations with his fists (and worse, with his shoes) is obviously "boorish." Why do these social judgments seem so *obvious?* Because we are seldom aware of our own norms; they are projected outward as the natural design of the universe.

Nor are we usually aware of the gradual drift of our own norms. It is always everything "out there" that is changing while we remain the bedrock of stability. It is always the younger generation that has changed, not us. Similarly, we have gradually adapted to the horrors of indiscriminate civilian extermination; now we can read with perfect calm that some general has been assigned the task of selecting strategic targets (cities) in Russia to be bombed if war comes, and the certain knowledge that some Russian general is busily pinpointing cities here hardly ruffles our deep complacency.

To appreciate fully the arbitrariness of our own norms it is necessary to get outside the framework provided by our own society, away from the pervasive cultural stimuli provided by our own mass media. Foreign travel is an excellent way to accomplish this, if you can break out of the "American bubble" that most of us carry around the world with us. During the past few years I have traveled in many countries in connection with cross-cultural research. I read the foreign press, to as great an extent as my linguistic talents would allow, and I found it full of refreshing heresy.

What does "being civilized" mean? It means more than having protected oneself from the vagaries of the environment with thermostats, refrigerators, and bathtubs. It means more than having a deep tradition in philosophy and religion. It means more than having harnessed electricity, magnetism, gravity, and the atom. It also means understanding the workings of one's own mind, so that its irrational tendencies can be recognized and controlled.

I think we can describe at least three stages in the process of becoming civilized inside. At the most primitive stage, *we unconsciously project our own norms onto others.* Since the Neanderthal in us naively assumes that everyone shares his norms, it must follow that if someone else sees as "straight" what to him is obviously crooked, calls "tasty" what to him is obviously distasteful, then this other person must be dishonest, evil, or at least abnormal in some way.

A classic example of this is given in Hans Reusch's novel about the Eskimo, *Top of the World*. The hero, Ernenek, plies his white guest with his most savory delicacies, like fermented bear brain, and is insulted when they are turned down in disgust. His wife, Asiak, makes the final gesture of Eskimo hospitality—prettying her hair with urine, greasing her face with melted blubber, and then offering herself to the guest, giggling and blushing. When the poor man tries to flee, Ernenek, outraged, dashes him against the wall of the ice hut until he is dead.

Primitive? Now look at the content of many radio broadcasts beamed to Russia. The Soviet citizens is told that he is the victim of a Communist conspiracy, slave to a system from which he receives no benefits; he hears that all people in the United States have equal rights (the Negro in the South is hardly mentioned); he is asked to believe that the Free World is strengthening its armed forces because of fear of *him;* he even hears his own Great Leader identified with Adolph Hitler, whom he hated and feared—and then Americans cannot understand why he calls it all propaganda. Of course, if the Voice of America were to try to understand the Russian citizen and then talk to him so that he *would* be impressed, Neanderthalic roars would resound from Capitol Hill.

The second stage is where *we recognize the relativistic nature of the other fellow's norms, but not our own.* This is the "forgive *them* for *they* know not what they do" kind of attitude, and at least it produces a more humanitarian approach to social problems. Members of minority groups are "pushy," "aggressive," or "immoral" because they happened to grow up under prejudice or without as much education and culture as we have had. This is the stage of the White Man's burden, and at least it leads to less punitive reactions than Ernenek's.

The third stage in becoming civilized is arrived at with difficulty and maintained with even greater difficulty. It is where *we recognize the equally relativistic nature of our own norms.* This is where a man tries to view objectively the nature and location of his own "platform" as well as that of others. This is the parent who can see that maybe his own idea of how high up the trousers should be to look right is really arbitrary. This is the sensitive—not "ugly"—American Peace Corps boy who realizes that his own norms for what is clean, tasty, and even moral are not necessarily any more natural or obvious than those of the Mexican or Hindu.

Accepting the idea of relativity in human social judgments is not the same as claiming there are no rights or wrongs, no goods or evils. In fact, it is just *because* human judgment is so liable to bias that we need to look continually for objective external criteria. The physical, biological, behavioral, and social sciences gradually provide such criteria—for physical and mental health, for population control, for growing better crops, or even for building better bridges.

Psycho-logic

It often happens in the human sciences that the results of research are heralded by common sense. A great deal of recent psychological research has been converging on a conclusion about human thinking that Ralph Waldo Emerson had already isolated with the statement, "A foolish consistency is the hobglobin of little minds." Unfortunately, the same hobgoblin rides big minds as well as little and in high places as well as low. Psycho-logic substitutes emotional consistency for rational consistency. It is the trademark of the Neanderthal mentality.

Here is how psycho-logic works. We carry around in our heads certain basic concepts that are definite goods or bads emotionally. Among the *goods* for most people are those we love and respect (like OUR PARENTS, OUR LEADERS, OUR FRIENDS, and, yes, OUR-

SELVES) and things we value (like AMERICA, GOD, and FREEDOM); among the *bads* are the people we dislike (like MURDERERS, DICTATORS, and OUR ENEMIES) and the things we dislike (like COMMUNISM, DISEASE, and SLAVERY). It is emotionally consistent for things and people we like to be associated favorably with each other (OUR FRIENDS should love AMERICA) and also for things and people we dislike to be associated favorably with each other (it "feels right" for COMMUNISM to be called SLAVERY). But it is not emotionally consistent for people we dislike to be favorably associated with things we like (it does not "feel right" to say COMMUNISTS love FREEDOM)—the people we dislike should be *against* the things we like, and vice versa (so it should be COMMUNISTS *hate* FREEDOM).

The Neanderthal within us is forever striving to force a complicated world into this oversimplified mold, in order to preserve for himself as simple and stable a world view as possible. To accomplish this, he is continually pulling and pushing ideas around in his head, distorting what he has heard or seen, shifting meanings to suit his feelings, and attributing motives and attitudes to others that they often do not have. Occasionally, of course, his psycho-logic happens to lead to logical conclusions, but this does not mean that the process itself is logical.

Thus, if we like JFK, and he happens to praise some diplomat from Afghanistan, we tend to feel favorably disposed toward this otherwise unknown individual. But let NIKITA comment on this same diplomat's sound ideas—a kind of association known as "the kiss of death"—and we suddenly find ourselves distrusting the man. I am reminded of a letter to the editor that appeared in my local newspaper. The writer said that a new directive of the Communist Party is to play up the dangers of nuclear war and generate a massive movement toward peace in the United States; he then asked if the readers realized that there were people at the University who were following this Communist line—who also were talking about the dangers of nuclear war and urging efforts toward peace. The letter was signed "Alarmed." One wonders what this alarmed Neanderthaler would do if Khrushchev were publicly to come out in favor of life!

Psycho-logic is the lowest common denominator of human thinking. It runs rampant in the area of international relations.

This is because the usual corrective process of *reality-testing* is hard to apply to people and things we have only met in the newspapers. In ordinary life, if a friend says he does not like X, and we therefore become set to dislike X also, we can be led to modify our opinion of X by meeting him ourselves—something hardly possible for most of us in international affairs. Thus, freed from the restraints of reality, psycho-logic in international relations runs wild. It is what leads many people to believe that Nehru must be pro-Communist when he insists on India's neutrality ("If he's not with us, he must be against us"). It has made bogey men of the opponents in every human conflict—the Simon Legree of the Civil War, the murderous Santa Anna of the Mexican War, the Kaiser of World War I, and the cruel, buck-toothed Jap of World War II—even though the same bogeys, not long before the war or soon after it, may have been our friends and allies.

What is the psycho-logic of bogey-building? Given the belief by each side that **we** are *good, kind, fair,* and so on—a necessary belief for mental health, and one that is generally true for every-day human relations—and given also the logical opposition be-tween WE and THEY, as between FRIEND and ENEMY, psycho-logic dictates that **they** must be *bad, cruel, unfair,* and so on through-out the opposites of all traits we attribute to ourselves. But what happens to this world view when we are exposed to real live THEYS—when we visit their homes and farms, or vice versa, and find them *friendly, sociable,* and in many ways *just like us?* The characteristic solution is to distinguish among the THEYS—it is the MEN IN THE KREMLIN who are the *bad, dangerous* fellows. And then, of course, the Neanderthal mind begins to wonder why the *good* RUSSIAN PEOPLE do not overthrow their *bad* COMMUNIST LEADERS (just as, no doubt, Ivan has been wondering why the *good* AMERICAN WORKERS, *just like him,* have not yet begun the revolution against their *bad* CAPITALIST LEADERS!).

Once the fundamental polarity between **we** and **they** is es-tablished, psycho-logic operates subtly but continuously on all subsequent incoming information. One effect is to push both sides in a conflict situation down opposing *paths of self-delusion.* Observe the alacrity and near-universality with which our media people jumped on the "Blame it all on Khrushchev" bandwagon even before the dust of the Paris Summit fiasco had settled, and even to the extent of claiming, in the face of clear evidence to the contrary, that Mr. K. had wanted to break up the meeting all along—while the Soviets, of course, were just as busily blaming it all on Eisenhower. Or witness the ease with which we accept as Communist-inspired any world event that displeases us; our susceptibility to such psycho-logic encourages every would-be dictator to cry "Communist wolf" every time he wants United States support.

Another effect of psycho-logic is the encouragement of *double standards of national morality*. Exactly the same behavior is moral if **we** do it but immoral if **they** do it. Why? Because different *motives* are attributed to us and to them in keeping with psycho-logic. Witness the debate in the United Nations over the U-2 incident: Americans, knowing themselves to be peaceful in intent but being afraid of treacherous surprise attack, viewed this as a legitimate defensive operation; Russians, knowing themselves to be peace-loving, not treacherous, but suspecting treacherous espionage from us, viewed this as a confirmation of their fears. Or observe the conclusion of an editorial in my local newspaper on the downing of a C-47 in East Germany: "It was not to be expected that the Americans would receive the courtesies and comforts showered upon those Russian sailors who . . . were rescued from their open boat . . . and given the grand tour in this country. There is satisfaction here that the C-47 incident had a happy ending, even if the Russians were actuated by propaganda motives and hope to profit from their action."

Many American travelers to Russia, including statesmen, scientists, and scholars, have been impressed by the *mirror image* of our own attitudes and beliefs they find there. Each side blames the other for the mutually aggressive relation. Each sees the other as untrustworthy and not sincerely desirous of peace; each sees the other as warlike, but itself as peace-loving. We explain our participation in the arms race as being due to our insecurity and fear of the Soviets; but, projecting our own self-image onto them, we cannot explain the Soviets' arms-building and testing as being due to their insecurity and fear of us—who could possibly be afraid of friendly, peaceful people like us?—so we must attribute it to their innate aggressiveness, their drive for power and self-aggrandizement, their inherent evil. And for the Soviets, we are the puppets of the "Capitalist warmongers" in Wall Street and the Pentagon, ready to cause war in order to preserve our decadent system and impose it on the world.

Now if we can recognize the falsity—as it certainly is—of the Soviet image of us, can we not admit at least the possibility of some bias in our image of them? It is amazing the tenacity with which the Neanderthal mind clings to its psycho-logic; to admit the possibility of bias in his image of THEM is to shake the very foundations of his whole world view.

We expect the normal human being to defend himself against attack, including mental attack. We expect him to deny the suggestion that he himself is in any way wrong or immoral. But we also expect him to be accessible to facts, pleasant or unpleasant. Both Russia and the United States, along with all other nations on the globe, have been steadily manufacturing their own versions of reality in absolute blacks and whites. As those of us who deal with individual humans under stress know so well, there are rarely if ever absolute blacks or whites. But in the behavior of nations we are asked to think like worms. When whole groups of people refuse to accept reality, when their communications media consistently paint self-righteous pictures, then there is no court to dispel the dangerous process of self-delusion. Both sides need thoughtful criticism from within, but the dynamics of Neanderthal thinking make such criticism hard to apply—or accept, once it has been applied.

Possibilism

Psychologists have known for a long time that there is a correlation between how confidently people expect something to happen and how strongly they wish or fear it would happen. This tendency is increased by the degree of emotional involvement in issues. When he is thinking calmly and rationally, Homo Sapiens bases his decisions on carefully estimated probabilities rather than upon mere possibilities. This is not true of paranoid schizophrenics, nor is it true of Homo Sapiens when he is thinking under stress. If the paranoid knows it is *possible* that his doctor belongs to the secret society persecuting him, he is likely to leap to the conclusion that his doctor *does* belong, and then the paranoid acts accordingly. Contrast this with normal decision-making: if I know that the probabilities of having an accident are greater while driving at night than in the day, I will drive more slowly at night, but I will not let the mere possibility of an accident keep me off the highways altogether.

Possibilistic thinking is one of the forces behind the arms race. If the WES know that the THEYS *could* be cheating, lying, or planning a surprise attack, it is easy to leap to the conclusion that the THEYS *are* doing these immoral things, and then, driven by psycho-logic, the WES are liable to do the same immoral things first in order to defend themselves, firmly proclaiming their motives to be benign.

In psychological experiments it has been found that the higher the stakes, the greater the potential rewards or punishments, the more possibilistic becomes decision-making behavior even though the odds remain the same. Exactly the same thing seems to be true in international decision-making; when the stakes are high, when a nation stands either to gain a great advantage or suffer a great loss, it is then that its decision-makers are most likely to act in terms of mere possibilities.

Stereotypy

The raccoon is a pretty intelligent little animal. Put him in a situation where he must discover which of several different doors will let him through to food and you will see him push first against one door, then against another, very flexibly, until he finds the one that opens up. Next time he will be more likely to come back to the door that worked before, but if it is not open this time, then back he will go to exploring other possibilities. But now excite the raccoon by putting him under a hot stinging shower while he is making his choice. He runs straight for the last door that *used to be open,* bangs his head against it—again, again, and again—paying no attention to wide-open doorways to left and to right.

If man is a cut above the great apes, he is certainly a good many cuts above the raccoon. Nevertheless, he displays the same relation between emotional tension and stereotypy of behavior. It is a basic fact about behavior that beyond some optimal level (at which behavior is maximally flexible and creative), further increases in tension reduce capacity for selecting among alternatives. Our most probable, habitual responses become relatively even stronger and our supply of weaker alternatives becomes even less available. When emotionally driven, our time span contracts toward the present moment, we see things in terms of most probable expectations, we decide things along most habitual lines, and our behavior becomes most predictable—in short, we become stereotyped, frozen.

One effect of tension-produced stereotypy is that *it reduces our capacity to solve problems*. What is a problem? It is a situation where the usual, dominant responses do not work; if they did, there obviously would be no problem. Just like the raccoon, humans are most creative and insightful in solving problems when they are operating under moderate levels of tension; put them under high tension and they tend to fall apart, become blind and stupid in their attempts to find a solution. Paradoxically, the greater the need for a novel solution the less likely we are to discover it. Up through the Neanderthaler, at least, Nature seems to have placed Her bets on habit as against insight.

Nations today are lumbering down the one habitual path to "security"—bigger and better weapons—gathering as they go tensions which make it less and less possible for their leaders to conceive of any other alternatives. Being traditional, this course of action is felt to be realistic. Unfortunately, anthropologists are only too familiar with societies that, through blind adherence to practices that once were realistic, have gradually committed suicide. I think we are in exactly the same spot; we are continuing to practice the rites and rituals of international relations that were developed in and appropriate to the past—firmly believing them to be realistic—in a nuclear present that renders them suicidal.

Another effect of heightened emotional tension is *loss of perspective*. As we trace the course of evolution and particularly the evolution of the cortex, we find that higher species have more extended foresight and are capable of striving for more remote goals. Within each species, more intelligent members display these characteristics more than less intelligent members. But emotional tension primitivizes this capacity. A monkey trained to delay opening a drawer for several minutes, until the proper signal is given, will, when made very hungry or frightened, grab for the drawer right away and thereby lose his peanut. Similarly, in this age of awesome weapons, the Neanderthal within drives us to grab for security *today*, however illusory it may be—and we also stand in danger of losing our peanuts.

Thus we find that the truly magnificent achievements of human science—achievements that may soon free us from earthly bondage and catapult us toward the stars—seem to have significance only within the petty framework of the cold war. The only question is, "Who's ahead?" We seem fixated on the immediate goal of staying ahead of our opponent in total military power, and no one in the mad scramble pauses to ask himself where all this is leading us. The larger goals of humanity and the civilization it has built together, not separately, are being lost in the scuffle. Like the anxious monkey, our obsessive concern for security today may cause us to lose all hope of security tomorrow.

THE NEANDERTHAL WORLD VIEW

What I have called the Neanderthal mentality is potential in all people, not just those with whom we happen to disagree. We are all susceptible to these ways of thinking, particularly when we are operating under emotional stress. Nevertheless, certain individuals display these characteristics more consistently than others. Whether we find them writing syndicated columns, making pronouncements in Washington, forming ranks with the Birch Society, or teaching eternal truths in academia, their views on foreign aid, on what we should do in Berlin, on the danger of Communist subversion from within, and on disarmament are highly predictable. Since the main resistance to any tension-reducing policy, like GRIT, will come from the Neanderthal within us, it behooves us to try to understand the world as it appears in his eyes. What follows is a caricature, overdrawn for emphasis, of the Neanderthal world view.

Projecting his own values onto others, he agrees with Al Capp that "what's good for Bull Moose is good for the country," and what is more, good for the world. Foreign aid should be used to keep people in line: given to those who agree with us and taken away from those who disagree with us or want to remain neutral. If they cannot see the obvious fact that ours is the best of all possible worlds, then why help them? This goes for the United Nations as well. As long as we can control it, and its votes go in our favor, we can tolerate it; but why should we continue to pay the lion's share of the bill for a United Nations that is not on our side? If necessary, we are powerful enough to go it alone.

His mind is oriented toward the past rather than the future— or even the present. If he had his way, he would repeal most of what has happened in the twentieth century and return to the friendly, familiar, and comfortable times of American self-sufficiency. He thinks of hydrogen bombs as just bigger and better clubs. He always prepares for the "next" of anything in terms of the "last" of anything in his experience. He prepared for World War II on the basis of his experience with World War I—and built a completely useless Maginot Line behind which he felt secure. And now he is preparing for World War III on the model of World War II—planning in terms of planes and ships, calling up reserves, and tightening his belt for a long period of sacrifice. He cannot conceive of a "war" that might be over in 48 hours.

Neanderthal thinking etches the world in absolute blacks and whites. Everything is channeled into the one overwhelming polarity of Free World good and Communist evil. Attributing power to an evil that justifies his fear of it, the Neanderthaler sees himself as being gradually encircled by a well-nigh omniscient enemy. Cuba is the closest and most threatening outpost of World Communism; he believes that Castro was trained as a Communist agent and that the revolution there was directed from Moscow.

He is therefore easily panicked by the dangers of a Communist conspiracy here at home, despite the insignificant size and political ineffectiveness of the Communist Party in the United States. Following the dictates of his psycho-logic, he believes that those who espouse views contrary to his own must be Communist-inspired. And thus, in the virtual absence of real Communists in his community, he creates his own legions of subversives—in the government, in the universities, and in the churches. He is completely oblivious to the fact that his noisy hunt for phantom witches at home seriously weakens our efforts to deal effectively with the real ones abroad, as J. Edgar Hoover has repeatedly pointed out.

Faced with such powerful and expanding evil on all sides, mounting anxiety narrows his perspective and robs him of his capacity to solve problems. He can think of only two alternatives:

keep applying the pressure and risk the chance of nuclear war or else show the signs of weakness which lead inevitably to surrender. And in this dilemma "I'd rather be Dead than Red," he says. He does not realize that this is a dilemma of his own making.

In every crisis, be it Cuba or Laos or Berlin, his position is inflexible toughness. This position is supported by several things. First, he believes that whenever good guys stand firm, bad guys back down (unlike his fare of television Westerns, where the bad guys *know* they are bad, in the real world of international politics the bad guys are equally convinced that *they* are good and that he will back down). Second, denying the dangers of nuclear war and being unable to comprehend what "60 million casualties" means in human terms, he actually believes that a war today can be won—that if they lose 100 million and we only lose 60 million, then we are the victors.

In the Neanderthal dictionary, "peace" has already become a sneer word. He equates it with "pacifist," which in turn means "coward"—all bad, weak, passive things. Drawing his own courage from the feeling that other people who count agree with him, he cannot comprehend courage which stands alone and out in the open. He is deeply distrustful of others and therefore has no real faith in negotiations; THEY will not keep their word, he says. Any step toward disarmament is thus seen as surrender, exposing him to danger; any compromise is seen as appeasement, and using Munich as his example, he says that to appease the tiger anywhere is to invite him in the door—except that appeasement in Munich did not in fact lead to ultimate surrender, as Hitler discovered too late. Any negotiated agreement requires that both sides be in favor of it, but Neanderthal psycho-logic requires that if THEY are for it, WE must be against it.

This, to be sure, is a caricature. It would be hard to find a real individual, even in the ranks of the Birch Society, who displayed all these characteristics. Nevertheless, it is an extreme toward which many of us are tending under the stresses of the cold war. I have been told that the same kind of thinking can be observed in the Soviet Union, and in even more virulent form. For the Russian Neanderthalers, old-line Stalinists and hard-line militarists, it is the Capitalists in the United States who are the dangerous tigers. It is these warmongers who, with underhanded tricks and soiled dollars, are manipulating people in the rest of the world like puppets, who are ringing the homeland about with military bases, who send agents in high-flying planes to spy on them, and who are just mad and desperate enough to bring the rest of the world down with them. Yet, being what they are, these Capitalists only understand force; there can be no appeasing them or compromising with them.

Now if the opponent is in truth entirely inhuman, there is no choice ultimately in a nuclear age but to kill *and* be killed. Or, if the opponent is actually much like ourselves, but we and he fail to see this and continue to hew blindly and inflexibly to traditional policies, then eventual nuclear holocaust is equally inevitable. There are ways of avoiding this future—by forging a different one. But it requires Homo Sapiens on both sides to understand and gain control over the Neanderthals within themselves.

OUR NATIONAL POSTURE

3

Our foreign policy is in a state of confusion. There is confusion between what we preach and what we practice. We preach peaceful intentions and willingness to negotiate but practice threat and inflexiblity in every crisis. We preach democracy but often practice support of dictatorship, suppression of popular revolution, and maintenance of colonialism. One reason for confusion is that the Homo Sapiens side of us does most of the preaching while the Neanderthal side does most of the practicing in crisis situations. Another reason for confusion is that we have assumed leadership of a Free World that is far from unified in its outlook. Yet another is that for many years our policy has been essentially reactive; frozen in a defensive pose, we have simply waited for challenges to be made by our friends or enemies, neither striving to create our own opportunities nor trying to anticipate approaching difficulties.

Nevertheless, we do have a national posture. It was not exactly planned this way; rather, we have been pushed into it by a combination of forces—including nationalism, the profit motive, Neanderthalism, and the nature of weapons in a nuclear age. The traditional response of a sovereign nation to external threat is to produce armaments for defense of the country. Producing armaments on an ever-expanding scale has created many very profitable enterprises which employ or indirectly support millions of people. The Neanderthal mentality provides a convenient rationalization for this profitable and prestigeful activity: THEY leave us no choice but to arm ourselves, and we must keep ahead in the race. But the grim reality of weaponry in a nuclear age—the fact that it is almost all offense and no defense—has made war unthinkable. The policy that has been forged inexorably by this combination of forces is called *mutual deterrence*. This policy is gradually making peace unthinkable, too.

One has the frightening phantasy of two towering war machines, red-banded East and blue-banded West, engaged in a ponderous danse macabre. Aggressive posturings of East are promptly mimicked by West, and vice versa, while the millions of little humans alternately cheer and groan for their champions. Are the people really in control of their war machines? Or has our military technology already achieved a mass and momentum with which ordinary human minds can no longer cope?

In his farewell address, President Eisenhower warned about the dangers inherent in the military-industrial complex. Human institutions have a way of developing their own self-generating and self-maintaining power, and the military institution is no exception. One might even ask if, in the consummation of this danse macabre, millions of American lives were traded for millions of Russian lives, would it really matter whose machine killed whom? Certainly not to the humans involved. Once missiles are on their way, theirs cannot be distinguished from ours; they wear no red or blue bands, and blast, fire, and radiation carry no signature. By taking persistent steps designed to reduce tension and mistrust, and by doing it in such a way as to induce the Soviets to reciprocate, we can gradually bring these war machines under control and begin to dismantle them; but it will not be easy.

THE MINIMUM REQUIREMENTS OF RATIONAL POLICY

If a society does not have a framework of long-term goals within which to set day-to-day policy decisions, it is likely to make them opportunistically to preserve whatever is the status quo of the moment. What are the goals of America? We all have a clear idea of what we are fighting against—Communism—but what are we fighting *for*? Certainly we do not want to annihilate other human beings for the sheer sake of killing. Nor do we want to impose our way of life on others, except as they observe our model and find it good. We have no need for expansion; we still have plenty of room to stretch here at home, so we do not want land in South America, Africa, or Asia.

What are we fighting *for*? For our principles and our lives. The simple truth of the matter is that we are afraid. We are afraid that the Communists are going to steal our freedoms and impose their system upon us; we are afraid that if we are not militarily strong, they will attack and destroy us. These are legitimate fears, and they establish two minimal objectives for policy in a nuclear age: (1) *we want to preserve our own way of life,* and to do this (2) *we must at least stay alive.* To these basic objectives we must add another, practical requirement: (3) *any policy must be feasible,* that is, must be workable within the existing setup of competing sovereign states.

There are really two quite different wars we must worry about. One is the danger of becoming involved in a *"hot" war with the Soviet Union as a sovereign nation.* This is the kind of war most people think about—full of soldiers and guns, military victories and defeats, destruction and death wreaked by each side on the other. World War III will not be quite like this; it will be full of death and destruction (as no other war has ever been), but there will be no time for marching bands or noble sacrifice. The criterion of sheer biological survival becomes uppermost here—we must prevent this war from happening. The other war is one that we have been waging for a long time; it is the *"cold" war with Communism* (and other totalitarian systems) *as an ideology.* It goes on steadily in the minds of men, and it is fought just as much within the borders of nations as across them, just as much here at home as abroad. This kind of war is the persistent attempt of one group of people to change the beliefs of another and make them conform to their own. It is here that the criterion of preserving our way of life becomes primary.

We stand in grave danger of losing the "cold" war simply by not waging it. For eight years, during which our decisions were dominated by John Foster Dulles' policy of "massive retaliation," we have been putting all our eggs in one atomic basket, busily preparing for a nuclear war nobody wants to fight. Meanwhile we have been steadily losing the real war with Communism as a way of life—by default. Despite what many people seem to think, victory in a "hot" war with Russia, even granting that winning in a nuclear war is conceivable, would not mean also winning the "cold" war with Communism. Indeed, winning an all-out nuclear war (in the sense of losing fewer millions of people than the Russians) would probably mean losing the real war with totalitarianism—by becoming a third-rate power ourselves under a tight military dictatorship.

But preserving our way of life, biological survival, and feasibility are only the minimal objectives of rational policy, and rather negative ones at that. There are many positive goals that could provide a framework for our international behavior. We like to believe that ours is the best of all possible worlds, but most people in most times have felt this way, too. Certainly, the future can improve on the present just as the present has improved on the past. We believe in equality of opportunity and justice for all men of all races and creeds; our policies should aim for this goal, both at home and abroad. We believe in raising standards of living, economically, socially, and culturally; our policies should aim for this goal, both at home and abroad. We believe in an international environment in which all nations, great or small, need no longer live in fear of external aggression or internal subversion; our policies should aim for this goal. There is much to be done.

Biological Survival

But first things first. I take the physicists at their word when they say that there is no real military defense against nuclear attack. I am impressed when I am told that one medium-sized thermonuclear bomb releases more destructive energy than all the ordinary bombs dropped on Germany and Japan during World War II. There are some who doubt that the coming of nuclear weapons has in any way changed "the old game of international politics." I ask them to try to hold in mind the *details* of shattered human bodies and plans, of disintegrating human culture and even protoplasm—and then listen to the estimate that in a full-scale nuclear attack we could expect by the sixtieth day 72 million dead and 21 million seriously injured, with only about 58 million relatively unscathed. Calculations based on comparatively minor and localized disasters—where people from completely intact surrounding areas have been able to come in and help—show that this proportion of survivors would not even be able to care for the injured or bury the dead, to say nothing of keeping a complex civilization going.

Threatening people with hell-fire without offering them any feasible solution merely reinforces complacency, it is true; the Neanderthal within simply denies the danger and goes on about "business as usual." Nevertheless, those concerned with the security of the nation can ill afford to minimize the threat to our biological survival these new weapons represent. Rather, they must hold this vision of hell-fire in focus while they strive to find ways to avoid it. Suffice it to say that without arms control, in the very near future warring nations will be able to destroy each other many times over. The availability of nuclear weapons with awesome capacities for destruction, to say nothing of chemical and biological weapons that are even easier to produce and harder to control, must be placed on the scales in evaluating any policy. If a policy does not clearly serve to reduce the likelihood of such weapons being used, it must be discarded and the search for something better continued.

Preservation of Our Way of Life

What is our American way of life? What distinguishes it from the Communist way of life? There are many differences, as any traveler will observe, but some of them are rather superficial, like the availability of luxury goods on the shelves, the number of automobiles on the streets, or the number of people reading books and attending concerts. The more critical differences all seem to reflect, in one way or another, *the relative freedom of individuals vis-à-vis their governments.*

The average American has much more freedom of choice than the average Russian as to what job he will have, whether he can strike or not, where and when he can travel, and so forth. Ivan takes it for granted that his government will plan things for him, and generally he trusts the decisions of his government and readily follows them. John, on the other hand, has a healthy distrust in government, particularly Big Government; his forefathers went out of their way to arrange things so that different parts of government would provide checks and balances with respect to each other. Where John considers it very dangerous for generals to indoctrinate their young troops with any particular political philosophy, Ivan takes it for granted that his generals are part of the political hierarchy. Perhaps most important, John has greater freedom of choice in getting different points of view in his education and in his mass media—if he exercises this freedom of choice.

Stripped to its essentials, the way of life we wish to preserve for ourselves and our progeny is one in which the state is relatively subservient to the best interests of the individuals who compose it. All of the things which dominantly characterize our way of life—a democratic form of government, a free enterprise economic system, a legal system which guarantees individuals equal rights to education and freedom of expression (including criticism of their own government)—seem to flow from this pervasive underlying notion. Even though practice may often fall far short of theory, the theory itself is most important. The development of this political philosophy, based upon the essential dignity of individual human beings, was a remarkable step along the path toward becoming civilized; it was both hard come by and all too easily lost.

The basic philosophy of Communism is quite the reverse of this. Stripped to *its* essentials, it holds that the individuals who compose the state are subservient to its best interests. The individual has no "rights"—to dissent, to be educated as he sees fit, to be fully informed, or to compete for as large a share of the economy as his talents and efforts will permit—except insofar as these things are viewed as serving the state. But again, practice does not jibe with theory. Just as technological and other developments have produced changes in our way of life—even though, being gradual, we often fail to recognize them—so are the technological revolution, universal education, and the race to catch up with the United States in material wealth gradually producing deviations from pure Marxist theory in the Soviet Union.

Although the cold war is waged in terms of rival theories, flexibility and rationality in foreign policy demand that we take account of how the two systems work in practice. There is evidence that common people throughout the world are steadily converging toward a common way of life, one in which they value political freedom, believe in relatively free economic enterprise, but side with the social and economic underdog. We will be wise not to let our psycho-logic create differences where there are none, or magnify differences that are minimal. The Russians do not see themselves as slaves; nor do they see Americans as free men. Both societies have been becoming increasingly conformist, although for quite different reasons; both have highly materialistic and technologically oriented cultures; both are aggressively competitive in their external relations. It is reported that Prime Minister Nehru of India once said that the two kinds of foreigners he had the most trouble telling apart were Americans and Russians!

Nevertheless, there remain fundamental differences between our way of life and the Communist way, both in theory and in the trend of practice. These real differences are extremely important to us, and any policy must serve to preserve our way rather than subvert it if that policy is to be acceptable.

Feasibility

There would be many alternatives available to us—if we were not the kind of creatures we are and if the world we live in were not just the way it is. By a feasible policy I mean one that humans as they are today would accept and pursue, one that, given the nature of the physical world and our technology, they *could* pursue. If some brilliant scientist were to come up with a technique for changing fissionable materials into inert lead, immediately and everywhere, then we might at one fell swoop eliminate the danger that nuclear weapons pose for our biological survival—but this seems most unlikely. If either the United States or the

U.S.S.R. were publicly to throw away all its weapons, it is probable that the other side would soon follow suit, and a more peaceful world would result—but this seems most unlikely.

It is not that "human nature" cannot be changed. It is very modifiable, given time. To be sure, people can hate and kill each other, given certain conditions; but they can also come to understand and help each other, given different conditions. It was not too long ago, as human history moves, that Protestants and Catholics were at each other's throats all over Europe, and no doubt there were many who cried "better dead than Papist," or something of the sort, and could see no alternative to unconditional surrender of one religion or the other. But following the Thirty Years' War there has been a gradual growth of religious tolerance and separation of church issues from state issues, until now people of different faiths live amicably side by side, and a Catholic can be elected President of a predominantly Protestant country like the United States. Wars between nations are no more inevitable than wars between other competing human organizations.

The question of feasibility arises not because of "human nature" but because of the particular shaping of it which we call *nationalism.* This is one thing that seems to be shared by all countries today, no matter how much they may differ in other respects. Among the external manifestations of nationalism are power competition and insistence upon the ultimate sovereignty of the nation state. Retaining the power of veto over decisions of the United Nations—which we decry when the Soviets use it but without which we would not participate—is a case in point. Among the internal manifestations of nationalism are intense emotional identification of individual citizens with national symbols; each national success or failure, no matter how insignificant, is felt as a personal reward or punishment. Nationalism imposes a hierarchy of values in which the status of one's own nation— its prestige, its power, and even its morality—takes precedence over everything else, including personal prestige, power, or morality. As a form of political organization, nationalism was an adaptive response to the technological developments of the past few centuries; it was one way of organizing ever-increasing numbers of people into reasonably stable political units.

But nationalism is no longer adaptive. Technological developments of the nuclear age have made some supranational form of political organization necessary as well as feasible. We are going to have to give up nationalism bit by bit; we are going to have to restrict our sovereignty in many areas—if we are going to be able to survive with the technology of a nuclear age. The failure of peoples and their governments to recognize and accept this fact fully is one of the deepest sources of resistance to rational policy. Every disarmament scheme, whether proposed by the Soviets or ourselves, requires gradual transfer of sovereignty from the nation state to some international authority. Limitation of national sovereignty is the price we must pay for international security.

But the fact remains that today nationalism, with all it implies about internation and intranation pressures, exists as the dominant political way of life. To be feasible, any policy proposal must take this state of affairs as given, must work within the limits of the situation created by nationalism, and yet must also serve to eliminate it gradually as the dominant form of political organization.

A HARD LOOK AT NATIONAL DEFENSE

Americans distrust Big Government and they dislike paying taxes to support it. Their elected representatives know this, and they snip, snap, and trim away at the budgetary requests of the Administration as a matter of course, be it for schools, for roads, for conserving our national resources, or for foreign aid. But there is one exception to this rule: expenditures in the name of "national defense" are not only approved by near-unanimous vote, but the gentlemen in Congress often add to the amounts requested. Why? They know that this is one place where Americans do not object to spending money or even to supporting Big Government. As a matter of fact, the biggest industrial giant in the nation today is not General Motors or American Telephone, but the Atomic Energy Commission. And who employs the most people? The United States government. The greatest expansion in Big Government has been the mushrooming of the Department of Defense and its many associated activities.

The dominant theme of American foreign policy for a long

time has been "peace through military strength." The only way to preserve peace and security in a threatening world, this theme goes, is to make ourselves so powerful that no nation or combination of nations would dare to attack us. Harmonized with this theme is the assurance that we will never use this terrible power unless provoked by aggression from outside. However, just what constitutes sufficient aggression from outside is never made very clear, so this theme and its harmony do more to support idealism at home than to calm anxieties abroad. This is still the basic policy of political and military leaders responsible for our security in a nuclear age.

But with a military technology that is nearly all offense and no defense, does our traditional posture of peace through strength still provide us with real security? Does the phrase "national defense" still have its old meaning? Since we are spending a great deal of money, willingly and even eagerly, for our defense, we have a right to know the answers to these questions; indeed, as citizens in a democracy we have an obligation to find the answers. Therefore, let us now evaluate our present policy against the minimal requirements we have established.

Biological Survival Through Military Strength?

In a world that has largely resolved itself into two competing blocs with roughly equal military power, "peace through strength" becomes "peace through fear of retaliation." And when thermonuclear weapons are placed on the scales, it soon becomes "peace through fear of annihilation." This is the foundation of our present policy of mutual deterrence. The hope is that with either side capable of practically wiping out the other with reflexive retaliation, a prolonged—if uneasy—peace can be maintained. What are the actual dynamics of this balance of terror?

One thing is clear enough. This is not a situation in which either John or Ivan can really feel secure. The incredible weapons still exist, with their looming threat to human life. In fact, it is the mutual terror itself that is supposed to guarantee the peace. Responsible officials on both sides, in government, the military, and science, feel as though they were tiptoeing about on atomic eggs. The consequences of one mistake, just one human error, have become almost incalculable. Furthermore, it is very difficult to keep up just the right degree of threat, not so little that an enemy is encouraged to attack through overconfidence and not so much that he is impelled to attack through fear. Over the long haul, this is an intolerable situation, both for nations and for the people who make them up.

The possibilities of *accidental war* are only too numerous. They have been cataloged in frightening detail by many writers of both science and science fiction. The absolute probability of accidental war may be small at any particular instant in time, particularly with the elaborate safeguards that have been devised for both men and materials, but this is no reason for feeling secure. The chances of throwing "snake-eyes" three times in a row may be very small, perhaps 1 in 50,000; but if you keep throwing dice over and over again, long enough, this particular rare sequence is certain to come up sooner or later. Similarly, the longer a state of mutual deterrence persists, the more and more likely becomes the eventual occurrence of a combination of events that will cause full-scale war. And the consequences of "triple snake-eyes" in this case are so catastrophic that no odds are really acceptable.

We had one very narrow squeak in October of 1960. At the Colorado Springs nerve center of the North American defense system (NORAD), manned jointly by Canadian and United States personnel, the newly installed Ballistic Missile Early Warning System (BMEWS), with immense radar installations in Greenland and elsewhere along our far-flung northern borders, suddenly began flashing signals of a multimissile attack coming from the general direction of the Soviet Union. *Snake-eyes no. 1.* The Canadian officer in charge gave the dread signal for war-alert, which put our retaliatory systems all over the world into readiness, but he withheld the signal for their release while frantic telephone consultations with the Joint Chiefs of Staff, and their equivalent in Canada, were held. Why? Because although there was evidence for missiles en route, there was no substantiating evidence of their ground firing. The NORAD center in Colorado tried to get in touch directly by telephone with the Greenland radar installation. Dead silence. As was discovered later, an iceberg had broken the cable. *Snake-eyes no. 2.* The Canadian officer held steady for nearly half an hour (which, had there really been an attack, could have been disastrous from a military point of view). Why? Because he knew that Khrushchev was at that moment at the United Nations in New York City, and it seemed most unlikely that he would be a Soviet sacrificial goat. There was no snake-eyes no. 3. By that time the explanation for BMEWS clicketing and clacketing about enemy attack became clear: it was nothing other than the powerful Greenland radar installation bouncing signals off the rim of the rising moon. But suppose some other officer had been in charge? Suppose Khrushchev had *not* been in New York? Suppose we had been in the middle of the Berlin crisis?

Today only two nations really have nuclear weapons and the means of delivering them. What happens as these capabilities spread to more and more countries? It is estimated that by 1970 at least ten countries will have nuclear weapons—unless controls are instituted. Just as the Colt 45 brought big men and little to common stature in the days of the Old West, so will nuclear (and biological and chemical) weapons become the "great equalizers" among nations. A Cuba armed with nuclear weapons and means of delivery *could* devastate the United States almost as completely as could Russia. The possibility of unintended war certainly must increase geometrically with the number of nations possessing nuclear weapons.

We cannot expect other nations to forgo the power over their neighbors and the illusion of security that these nuclear equalizers seem to offer. To the contrary, we can expect them to beg, borrow, and steal the necessary know-how and materials. There is increasing pressure from West Germany for the United States to release control of nuclear weapons to the NATO forces, including the Germans—a move which would have a dangerously unstabilizing impact upon our relations with the Soviet Union. Furthermore, since the source of even an ICBM attack would be difficult to pinpoint in the short time available—to say nothing of the source of a "suitcase" attack—it becomes possible for an aggressive nth power to touch off a full-scale nuclear war between the major powers. Then, surely, would the meek inherit the earth—or what is left of it.

The responses of nations to such a situation of external danger and conflict are complex and varied, but they are all aimed at trying to increase national security. The traditional response is to demand research, development, and stockpiling of newer and better armaments. Spokesmen for the several military services, for military science, and for the industries which supply them have become very adept at "crying wolf" when budgetary decisions are being made. The public's memory is not quite long enough to recall that the voices that yesterday were boasting that "we can destroy anyone who dares to attack us" are the same that today are complaining that "we are dangerously behind," and who tomorrow will again be declaring that "we are the most powerful nation on earth." Missile gaps have a strange way of shrinking and expanding with the propaganda demands of the moment, whether for increasing appropriations or for facing down an opponent. But every step that serves to increase security at home serves to decrease security abroad. The policy of mutual deterrence thus leads inevitably to an armament race.

This inevitability is *not* rational; being able to annihilate an enemy ten or even a hundred times over probably deters him little more than simply being able to annihilate him once. Rather, it is psychological. Brown and Real, in their *Community of Fear*, have characterized the competitive psychology of the arms race in this way: "Can gigaton bombs be built? We must do the work and see. Can climate over the Soviet Union be altered? We must experiment. Can the earth be burned, broken, kept from rotating? . . . All these questions must be considered. If we don't consider them, the Russians might, and if successful they would have us at a disadvantage." Thus, driven by human suspicions and anxieties, the arms race is not the poised balance of deterrence that mathematicians and chess players are fond of envisaging. It is, to the contrary, a highly volatile, teetering imbalance in which either side may believe itself so far behind as to strike out defensively, or so far ahead as to strike out offensively.

The Russians have already exploded a 50-megaton bomb, and Khrushchev has talked about testing a 100-megaton dandy—which would probably be capable of obliterating all of Rhode Island in one strike. No doubt they were driven by the same forces that impel our own military—a combination of bluff and fear. Both sides are caught in the same blind alley of trying to achieve "peace through military strength."

The final surrender of our right to decide our own fate is to be found in proposals for a "push button for the dead man's hand" and for a "Doomsday machine." We must have automatic devices that will react to blast, heat, or radiation and release our retaliation, the argument goes, because a sneak attack might well wipe out most of our military personnel. And there being no apparent limit to the size of nuclear weapons, a "Doomsday machine" would be the final guarantee of mutual suicide—a deeply buried device capable of literally fragmenting the planet, or a high altitude shot that would radiate the whole surface.

The purpose of such nuclear devices, of course, is to deter, and the assumption is that they never will be used; but as long as they exist, is it possible to talk rationally about their guaranteeing our biological survival? The basic truth remains: the only real defense against nuclear weapons is their elimination.

Preserving Our Way of Life Through Military Strength?

Even though we have the initial advantage of a broadly based industrial economy, our way of life ill fits us for prolonged deterrence and the arms race it engenders. A totalitarian system seems better able to wage a conflict on these terms than a democratic system. Where the Communists have been able to channel the energies of their people into heavy industry and weapons production at the expense of civilian comforts, we have been trying to maintain both a massive military establishment and the luxury civilian economy advertised by Madison Avenue. Where the Communists have been able to order their young people into mathematics, engineering, and the physical sciences, our democratic system allows youths to choose their own careers—and most of them choose the business world, where our free economy provides the biggest rewards. Where the Communists are able to make quick decisions and abrupt reversals of policy without reference to the will of the people, democracy requires the consent of the governed and therefore displays greater inertia. It would seem, then, that to pursue this policy successfully will require us to give up as quickly as possible beliefs and practices that hamper us in the race.

Signs of erosion of our way of life are already becoming apparent to those with eyes to see, despite the gradualness of the process. Maintaining deterrence demands a unified front, so the very diversity of opinion on which democracy thrives becomes dangerous (and we find one presidential candidate condemning the other for debating foreign policy while Khrushchev is at the United Nations). The arms race demands secrecy, so the information citizens need in order to govern themselves intelligently is kept from them (and the press tries, usually in vain, to pierce through the thickening fog). Maintaining balance on the slippery seesaw of an arms race demands quick decisions, so we see steadily increasing pressures to sidestep the democratic process (and policy-executing agencies like the AEC and the military begin to assume policy-making roles, while elected representatives of the people tend to stand by and merely rubber-stamp their decisions).

Whether or not one considers these changes in our beliefs and practices necessary under present world conditions, they nevertheless represent a pervasive weakening of our democratic institutions. Some will argue that it has always been necessary to give up our freedoms in time of war in order that, in the long run, we might preserve them. But the real war being fought right now is an ideological one, and it has no foreseeable conclusion, at least not in our own lifetime. After all, our "way of life" is nothing more than a set of learned habits of thinking and behaving, and they can just as easily be unlearned and forgotten by another generation. Prolonged subjection to a totalitarian set of beliefs and practices, *particularly and perhaps only if self-imposed*, will result in a thorough distortion of our own principles.

These are some of the effects of prolonged deterrence within; what about the effects elsewhere? The belief to which Dulles clung in the face of contrary evidence, and to which many still cling today, is that the Communist system will somehow naturally "crack" if the stalemate persists and we keep increasing the pressure. It is true that there are now operating in Russia and the satellite countries strong liberalizing forces. These became most evident in the shift from Stalinism to the present regime. These forces have been generated by universal education, by a gradually expanding civilian economy, by an increasingly self-conscious technological "midde class," and other developments. But the external threat created and maintained by the arms race has just the reverse effect to what Dulles expected: it serves to "keep the totalitarian cap on" and it strengthens the hand of those who believe that war with the Capitalist imperialists is inevitable. Why? Because the perception of external threat creates precisely those conditions under which individual human beings are willing to forfeit their rights for the good of the state and sacrifice both physical luxuries and intellectual freedoms.

There are other, more subtle, psychological effects of prolonged nuclear deterrence. Continued exposure to statistics on the destructiveness of hydrogen bombs, to bellicose threats to use them, and to continuing tests of their power—coupled with statements that there are no alternatives to war or surrender—is creating widespread indifference to the prospect of war and equally widespread callousness to the mass extinction of human lives. Our historical perspective is becoming compressed into the immediate here and now. How many of us have said to ourselves, when someone mentions a long-term goal, "We should live that long." This compression of time-perspective is accompanied by a shrinkage in our humanitarianism; we are becoming more selfishly concerned with what is good for us and less altruistically concerned with the welfare of others.

I do not have the facts as yet, but I suspect that the same impacts are being felt by our children. Do our teen-agers plan as far ahead as we used to do—for what they will do in college, for what they should place securely in their hope chests, for what role they will play in the world's work? And has anyone looked closely into the phantasy worlds of our children—at their drawings, at their stories, at the content of their games? Are the images more somber and the themes grimmer? Is grayness replacing golden yellow, is disorder conquering order? I do not know.

But I do know that in the superficially logical pursuit of peace through military strength we are losing sight of the prime goal of a military establishment, its only justification for existence in a democracy: the defense of our national values, ethics, and institutions. We must ask our military leaders some very simple questions: What and whom are you defending? Do civilians exist to defend and preserve the state, or does the state exist to defend its civilians and preserve their way of life? We must ask these simple questions again and again—and demand the right answers. Prolonged mutual deterrence fosters the very conditions, both in the United States and in Russia, which support totalitarian values and ways of life. In a most basic sense, then, this is a weapon turned against ourselves. By pursuing this policy we may be losing what we are really fighting for in the course of fighting for it.

How Feasible Is "Stabilized Deterrence"?

Even if we were willing to sacrifice our way of life in order to stay alive, by pursuing the policy of mutual deterrence into a long, unforeseeable future, is this a feasible course for the United States? If man can be assumed to be a perfectly rational animal—an assumption I will challenge in just a moment—then the answer to the question of feasibility would seem to come down to whether we think of mutual deterrence in terms of the minimum necessary or in terms of an ever-expanding arms race. Certainly it is feasible in the near future for this country to develop a system of "hardened" intercontinental missile bases, as well as mobile Polaris submarine bases, that would be well-nigh impregnable. As a matter of fact, given the forces at work, this is almost certainly going to happen on both sides, and therefore it must be taken into account in any serious policy proposal. Such a minimum capacity for certain and unacceptable retaliation would satisfy the requirements of deterrence.

But, as we have seen, competitive military psychology leads far beyond the minimum necessary for effective deterrence into the continually expanding seesaw of an arms race. Is it possible for this country to hold a favorable balance in such a race? In my own attempt to weigh this question objectively I am forced to the somber conclusion that we would ultimately fall behind in this kind of competition if extended over many decades.

Why? We have already considered how our way of life as a democratic society ill fits us for this kind of race. But there are other reasons. Ours is the smaller nation in terms of both area and manpower, particularly if we place Communist China on the scales. Our natural resources have been more fully used to date than have those of China and the Soviet Union. Our traditional isolation by virtue of the two great oceans that have separated us from potential enemies of the past has lost its meaning in an age of intercontinental missiles. We used to be supremely confident in our greater supply of educated young people, our greater mastery of science, and our greater technical know-how, but surely now only those who have been incapable of reading the signs in our skies hold this confidence unshaken. The more mutual deterrence is prolonged, the less will become our advantage. Obviously, this puts pressure on our military strategists—to stop being deterred.

But can mutual deterrence be maintained over a long period without something happening? What if man is *not* a perfectly rational animal? National policy-makers and their consultants have begun to inquire soberly into the question of just how stable "stabilized deterrence" can be. Just because we now have this metallic-sounding phrase—which surely suggests the existence of some hard, protective technological shell of defense about us—does not mean that there is really something "out there" in the real world that corresponds to the phrase. There is no defense in mere words.

I will state flatly that deterrence is more a psychological question than a technological answer. An opponent is assumed to be deterred from initiating a nuclear attack by his expectation of unacceptable retaliation. But if the opponent is not deterred, if he makes a wrong decision—whether due to fear, to overconfidence, to misinformation, or even to some accident—then all of the invulnerability of our retaliatory capacity and the certainty of its delivery does nothing whatsoever to defend our own civilians from his first strike. This is why some Americans are now seriously considering digging themselves into holes. This is also why learned discussions of stabilized deterrence keep coming down to questions about the "credibility" of our deterrent and about the "rationality" of human decisions—which, surely, are psychological matters.

Yet most of these discussions take off from the unquestioned assumption that man *is* a rational animal. Is he? Always? In the last chapter we peered into a dirty mirror and saw the Neanderthal within us staring back. We know that it is under emotional stress that he tends to take control. So now let us confront some of the necessary assumptions for "stabilized deterrence" with some of the psychological facts about human decision-making under stress.

Credibility of deterrence assumes full appreciation of the dangers of nuclear war on both sides. It is this deeply felt threat which is supposed to prevent the launching of an attack. But the mechanism of denial, the refusal to accept consciously and keep in mind an overwhelming threat, the perverse compulsion to flirt with the very danger denied, and the essential meaninglessness of the words we use to talk about it all—all these things operate to make us depreciate and forget the magnitude of the danger. The longer the threatening situation persists, unchanged and apparently unchangeable, the more we come to disregard it.

Stability of deterrence assumes objective evaluation of the intentions of an opponent and objective interpretation of world events. So as not either to overreact or underreact to enemy moves or to events elsewhere in a complex world, we must observe through clear glasses and interpret with clear minds. But both our psycho-logic, which transforms the complexities of international relations into an oversimplified television contest between the good guys and the bad guys, and our tendency to project our own values and beliefs onto others hinder such objectivity. We do not see the real world or the actual motives of people in it, but rather an Alice-in-Wonderland world of our own fancies, filled with trick mirrors and phantoms that move with purposes of our own devising. Prolonged deterrence cannot be maintained when both sides are balancing themselves as much against phantoms as against real men.

Stability requires that decisions be based upon accurate estimation of probabilities rather than emotional reaction to mere possibilities. If, unlike our rational Canadian officer in charge of NORAD when the moon illusion occurred, decision-makers were to react in terms of mere possibilities—to an accidental explosion in terms of the certainty that it means an enemy attack, to a Soviet bluster in terms of the certainty that it means a take-over in Berlin, to a seismic disturbance in terms of the certainty that it means clandestine testing or launching—then deterrence would be a flimsy thing indeed. Psychologists know that the wishful-fearful thinking characteristic of paranoid schizophrenics also colors the judgments of normal people, particularly when they are functioning under stress. They become prone to deciding in terms of their wishes (overconfidence) or their fears (underconfidence). And we should not forget that there are many truly irrational people in the world. Even though there are more hospital beds for mentally ill people than for any other disorder, there are still many not in such beds. Some of these people have suicidal tendencies, and in destroying themselves when thwarted, have no compunction whatsoever about destroying others. The stress of prolonged deterrence could be expected to increase the numbers of such people, in high places as well as low.

Maintaining stable deterrence in a world where situations change with bewildering speed demands great flexibility of means coupled with equal consistency of ends. To respond effectively to probes and ploys in the cold war that accompanies deterrence, we need to have a set of long-term goals to guide us and a diversified set of tactics to accomplish them. But, as we have seen, emotional tension produces stereotypy in our thinking; it restricts the range of alternatives we can conceive of, rendering us more rigid than flexible, and shortens our perspective, substituting blind reactions to immediate pressures for long-term persistence toward ultimate goals. In other words, paradoxically, the psychological conditions of prolonged deterrence produce the very states of mind which make it harder and harder to maintain deterrence.

Now it is true that men can be rational, and they often are; but it is also true that they can be irrational, and they often are. These are only some of the mechanisms of nonrationality. These are only some of the ways in which humans reach decisions without the benefit of logic and without even maximizing their own self-interest over the long run. Yet these ways of thinking are lawful, in the sense that they do conform to and are predictable from the principles of human behavior. In the situation presented us by the nuclear age, where one single bit of irrationality could set a whole train of traumatic events in motion, I do not think we can afford to be satisfied with the assurance that "most people behave rationally most of the time."

ARMS CONTROL AND TENSION CONTROL

What are the conditions that strengthen and exaggerate these nonrational mechanisms in human decision-making? What conditions serve to make normally normal people appear irrational— and, we must add, serve to make truly irrational people appear normal? Under analysis it seems that the same conditions that make normals seem irrational also make irrationals seem normal. To a population driven into a high level of emotional tension, as with the Germans in the period following World War I, a fanatic like Hitler may appear not only normal but ideal.

Military and political strategists are very much interested in the answers to these questions. This is because one of their primary concerns is with the "stability of the military environment" —which means many things, including the predictability of human decisions in this environment. One way of stabilizing the military environment is through the practice of arms control by both sides.

"Arms control" is another term which has an interesting history and usage. Military men for the most part do not like to talk about, or even think about, "disarmament"; it has a decidedly unmilitary ring to it (and even smacks of technological unemployment). On the other hand, most military men are sensitive to the dangers of nuclear war and to the paradoxes of the age in which they find themselves. Let us face the fact that a 48-hour war that leaves no time for promotions and perhaps not even any society that needs or wants his services is not a soldier's cup of tea! But the term "arms control" has a different character altogether; it has a taut trimness about it, and it also seems to imply clearly that the role and status of the military will be maintained. If this means some kind of implicit agreement with the opponent's military—well, after all, we can understand another military mind and do business with it. So the Pentagon talks about "arms control" while the State Department talks about "disarmament."

There are two general sets of conditions that affect the rationality or nonrationality of decision-making, and hence could influence the stability of the military environment through arms control. The first of these concerns *information*—its availability, bias, and overload in the human decision system. The second concerns *tension level* and its dynamic relation to the mechanisms of thinking we have been discussing.

Information

The sheer magnitude of nuclear weaponry, the diversity of its deployment, the political complexity of its use, and the incredible speed of its delivery have put a high premium on the accuracy and rapidity of processing military information. This is why we have far-flung electronic nets about us for early warning with intricate computers attached to them. This is why we have many scientists and engineers struggling to devise ever more complicated man-machine systems to bring together and synthesize information from all over the globe. When time is so short and risks are so great, we cannot afford to hold lengthy conferences and public debates to arrive at a democratic decision; this must come *before* the critical event.

But even all this is not enough. As the speed with which missiles can be delivered increases, the response time for effective retaliation decreases; and as retaliation response time decreases, so does the time for rational thought and considered action. Elaborate early warning systems, at best, can give but a little more time, and in themselves they represent no defense (much popular nonsense in the media to the contrary). Further, despite the sensitivity of our far-flung net, the information we get is always incomplete, and what is relevant is often hopelessly confounded with what is irrelevant. Even rational men are unable to reach rational decisions when the information they have is insufficient or biased—the abortive Cuban invasion attempt is probably a case in point.

It is also true that anything that overloads the input to a human decision-maker reduces his rationality. He begins to miss certain bits and overemphasize others, or he may even freeze mentally. Overload of this sort can be caused by increasing the speed of information input (for example, during a possible attack), by increasing the amount of information that must be processed (for example, as the number of countries that must be watched goes up), or by decreasing the time for final decision (for example, knowing that he has only ten minutes to reach a fateful choice). Computers can help humans under such conditions—by organizing, relating, integrating, and synthesizing all the thousands of bits of data into larger chunks—but, unless we want to surrender ourselves completely to the decisions of electronic brains, some humans somewhere in the complex system have to put it all together and make choices.

Furthermore, there are ever-increasing complexities in what is called "command and control." As the time available for decision goes down, there must be greater dispersion of decision-making away from central authority toward more and more people whose fingers are closer to the critical buttons. After all, we would not care to be caught in the situation where a carefully contrived and timed set of assassinations in the White House and the Pentagon rendered our entire military machine headless and incapable of effective response. To some degree and under some conditions, then, subordinate decision-makers—the captains of Polaris submarines and the colonels in charge of Minutemen sites, for example—must have autonomy. And to this degree we must worry about *their* sources of information, *their* understanding of the total world situation, and *their* emotional stability. Inevitably, as autonomy in decision-making spreads to more and more individuals, the chances increase that it will touch someone who is psychologically unstable.

Tension Level

We have already seen that beyond some optimal level for alertness, further increases in tension restrict a person's range of perceived alternatives, thereby limiting his flexibility and creativity in solving problems. It is also certainly true that increasing tension beyond some optimal level serves to magnify the ratio of irrationality to rationality. Under great stress a man becomes more likely to strike out blindly or even freeze into stupid immobility.

In other words, both flexibility and rationality in human thinking "ride on the back" of general tension level. This relation is shown graphically in the accompanying diagram. There is some optimal level of tension (point b) at which a person displays the greatest range of available alternatives and little likelihood of acting irrationally. As tension level builds up beyond this optimum, the range of possible alternatives a person can conceive of narrows (the width of the envelope) and the proportion of these alternatives that are likely to be irrational increases.

World events may have either a tension-increasing or a tension-decreasing impact upon the international system. This is shown in the diagram by the arrows attached to the location points. Attempts by East German police to obstruct the movements of NATO military personnel through the corridors has a tension-increasing impact; a statement by Khrushchev that a separate treaty with East Germany will be delayed has a tension-decreasing impact. *The real stability of the international system depends upon its capacity to absorb such event-shocks, and this in turn depends upon the absolute level of tension.* If the system

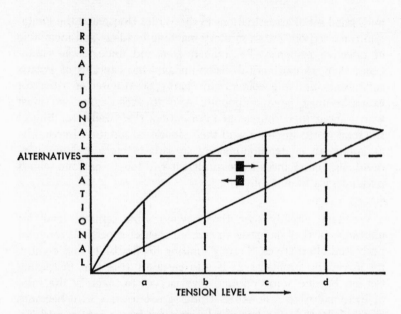

is functioning at a relatively low level of tension (point a), it can absorb a succession of tension-increasing event-shocks—such as a revolution in some South American country, the demonstration of a new weapon, or the accidental explosion of an old one—without being shifted out of the region of optimal flexibility and rationality. But if the system is already functioning at a high level of general tension (point c)—for example, during the Berlin crisis—then exactly the same set of event-shocks could easily push it over into the dangerous region of rigidity and irrationality. And, of course, a system at point d is explosive. It should also be noted that a system at point b may be optimum for creative problem-solving, but it is not optimally stable.

The sources of tension may be events external to a nation—for example, a stepping up of the bombardment of Quemoy and Matsu or the discovery of a high ratio of first-strike to second-strike capability in the arsenal of the opponent. But the sources of tension also may be internal to a nation—for example, arising in the privations of an economic depression. They may even be internal to the individuals within a nation—for example, the frustration felt by military personnel under inaction when they are unable to fulfill their functions. Tension level varies with the prediction of future power relations between one's own nation and an opponent, even though such predictions are largely subjective and readily influenced by momentary successes or failures of policy. Losses or gains in national prestige also affect tension level; in fact, the momentum of past decisions, as with respect to China and the United Nations, may create high tensions when reversal of policy is even considered.

It is important to realize that tensions cumulate over various events, even though the effect upon flexibility and rationality is quite independent of the source. Equally important for the policy proposals I will make later is the fact that *reduction* of tension is independent of its sources and can be accomplished by means that are unrelated to them. Tensions generated by events in Cuba and Laos were damped somewhat by the talks between President Kennedy and Premier Khrushchev at Vienna, for example. As a matter of fact, the tension-increasing or tension-decreasing impact of events may be all out of proportion to their military significance—witness the way Sputnik I increased tensions in the United States without shifting in any significant degree the balance of military power. In other words, tension level is something like money in a bank account: its amount can be increased by "deposits" from a variety of sources and decreased by "withdrawals" for a variety of purposes.

If this analysis of the relation between "stability of the military environment" and tension level is valid, then it obviously puts a high premium on devising and applying *techniques of tension control*. Stability is a dynamic concept, not a static one, and we need to create and maintain a dynamic, shock-absorbing "cushion" for the international system. If I can read between the lines in the reports that both President Kennedy and Premier Khrushchev made to their peoples after the discussions at Vienna, one of the few points of agreement was that tensions must somehow be controlled so that disaster through accident or miscalculation can be avoided. This was good, because one of the most unstabilizing factors in our present situation is the suspicion of irrationality that each side has of the other. Unfortunately, subsequent actions by both sides in Berlin have not confirmed their words with deeds. In any case, there remains the problem of method; how can international tension levels be reduced and controlled?

In one of the possible futures for man with which we began this book, a way of reducing and controlling tensions was outlined. Under the firm leadership of the President, the United States began taking the initiative with small but steady steps designed to reduce tension and distrust. The early moves were met, as would be expected, with skepticism abroad and emotional resistance at home, but the policy was kept going. Before internal resistance forced the President to give up the "March Toward Peace," the Soviets began reciprocating in clearly bona fide ways, and then internal resistance to the policy began to crumble. This was only a hypothetical future, to be sure, but it is a possible one. In the remainder of this book I shall try to make this possibility more real, first by showing that something of this kind may be our only viable alternative in a nuclear age and second by detailing the nature of GRIT and its strategy.

THE ULTIMATE POLICY QUESTION

Our political and military leaders have been virtually unanimous in their public support of the "peace through military strength" policy and in their assertions that we must get ahead and stay ahead in the arms race. But by every single one of our basic requirements, this policy is unacceptable. Rather than eliminating the threat to our biological survival, the policy of mutual deterrence and the arms race it engenders keep nuclear weapons around ever ready to be launched, and continue to improve on their destructive capacity. Rather than serving to support our democratic way of life, this policy creates conditions under which totalitarian beliefs and practices flourish, both here at home and abroad. Rather than meeting the criterion of feasibility, it has been shown that prolonged deterrence is almost inconceivable, given the unstable psychological ingredients on which it depends. Yet right on down the same old rut we keep pounding, driven by the Neanderthaler on our back.

Our political and military leaders have been equally unanimous in saying absolutely nothing about when and how mutual deterrence ends. This is the ultimate policy question. Let us even suppose that by some frantic balancing act we were able to maintain something like stabilized mutual deterrence. What happens then? There we would poise, on our hardened land bases and elusive submarines, each with the capacity to annihilate the other completely. Do we remain in this unsteady equilibrium forever? *The policy of mutual nuclear deterrence includes no provisions for its own resolution.* No one in the heat of the arms race asks the obvious next question: When and how does all this end? Surely a policy that, at best, can offer us nothing more than a world poised everlastingly for mutual destruction, kept from it by nothing more than fragile psychological reeds of mutual fear, must not be the last word.

ALTERNATIVES

4

There is a lot of loose talk these days about our only choice lying between being "Red or Dead." This is pure, unadulterated Neanderthalism. It tries to take the great complexities and difficulties of our time and squeeze them into two tight little boxes. It is foolish talk, because the people who pose this question want to be *neither* Red nor Dead. What they mean to say is that our only choice lies between surrender to the Communists' way of life or getting tougher and taking the chance of becoming dead in a nuclear war. More than foolish, this is dangerous talk. It is the kind of stereotyped thinking that puts a lid on creative thinking and encourages fatalistic acceptance of nuclear war as a tolerable alternative.

I do not know just who it was who first coined the thought-stopping phrase "Red or Dead," but the underlying issue was crystallized in a debate between Bertrand Russell and Sidney Hook on the pages of the *New Leader* in the summer of 1958. Lord Russell maintained that a Communist victory in the cold war would certainly not be so great a disaster as the extinction of human life in a hot war. Hook maintained just the reverse; for him, death in a nuclear holocaust would be preferable to life under the Communist system. If this were our only choice, I, for one, would have to side with Bertrand Russell in this calculus of human values; not only is survival a minimum requirement for achieving any other, more lofty goal, but in life there is hope. Good ideas are hard to kill as long as there are men around to cherish them. And, furthermore, is it not more than a little arrogant for a mere handful of men of only one generation to make such a grim decision for all people and for all time?

But—fortunately—this is *not* a decision we are called upon to make at this time. And if we keep our wits about us, we will never be forced to choose between Red or Dead. Those who pose the policy problem as a choice between abject surrender to Communism or continuing as we are going to the point of no return have already given up trying to solve it; they have stopped thinking. Homo Sapiens is a creative, inventive creature. Right now he needs social inventions to match his technological innovations. We need to continue the search for fresh policy alternatives, strategies that will enable us both to survive *and* to preserve our own way of life. Russell and Hook, brilliant scholars though they may be, have done their species a disservice, I think, by posing the policy issue in such all-or-nothing terms.

DRIFT

The easiest alternative in any problem situation is just to keep on doing what comes naturally. This demands the least effort, the minimum of hard, new thinking. This is the alternative into which those who practice denial fall ("What's everybody so worried about?"). They see us as somehow standing forever frozen in the national posture of peace through military strength. They do not ask themselves—as we had to do in the last chapter—when and how this all ends. They do not question the stability of "stabilized deterrence," because to do so would be to shake the very foundations of their sense of security. They contribute willingly to the arms race, but fail to see in it the seeds of ultimate destruction. They greedily accept a phrase like "balance of terror," remembering the "balance" but forgetting the "terror," while they complacently go about living their everyday lives in an everyday fashion.

It is interesting that today many highly sophisticated and intelligent men—particularly those whose professional activities are supported directly or indirectly by the military establishment—are saying that we no longer need worry about a nuclear war because we have had the weapons for ten years now and no war has broken out. This is a strange kind of reasoning. People had lived for hundreds of years in Pompeii at the foot of Vesuvius and it had never erupted—but one day it did. A full eclipse of the sun by the moon has not happened in Chicago for some time—but it will, when the conditions are right. The mere fact that something has not yet happened does not necessarily make it less likely to happen, particularly if a critical combination of conditions is required for that something to occur. After all, it has only been for a few years that the U.S.S.R. has had even rough parity with the United States in nuclear weaponry. As long as these weapons exist and there is neither defense against them nor control over them, men being what they are and gadgets being what they are, wrong decisions can be made and accidents can happen.

During the period when the United States had a virtual monopoly over nuclear weapons, and "massive retaliation" was our basic policy, if anyone dared to displease us, we threatened literally to blast him off the face of the earth. Not only was this threat clearly not designed to win friends and influence people, it was sheer nonsense. It was like a man saying he would use dynamite to get rid of the mice in his house. Massive retaliation is obviously something to be used only as a last resort; only if our heartland itself were endangered, only if our very survival were threatened, would we be willing to unleash such a holocaust. Both our allies and our enemies knew this—the former finding little comfort in it and the latter little real threat—so the policy had minimum credibility, and the mice continued to nibble away. The threat of massive retaliation is completely unwieldy as an instrument for dealing with the everyday skirmishes of foreign policy that have less than survival significance.

If we were inhibited by self-restraint from using nuclear weapons when we had a virtual monopoly over them, we are now doubly inhibited in a situation where there is an unstable parity in nuclear weapons and retaliation is almost a certainty. With nothing positive to offer by way of foreign policy, this situation of mutual deterrence has created a *Great Freeze on initiative.* Our posture is largely defensive and reactive. We do not dare to do anything boldly—except talk—for fear of starting something we might not be able to finish. To borrow an apt phrase from Robert Colborn, an editor of *Business Week,* our international relations now display the massive apathy of people moving about under water. While we wait passively for our opponents to do something significant enough to warrant the kind of response we are keyed for, the mice keep nibbling away and all we can do is react defensively. As long as we have no policy framework within which to take the initiative, we will continue to drift until forces not of our own choosing decide the thing for us.

WAR AS USUAL

The flat failure of deterrence through massive retaliation to provide a workable framework for everyday international behavior has led some people to search for ways in which ordinary war could be retained as an instrument of foreign policy. Proposals have taken one of two general forms. One is to seek explicit promises or implicit agreements to ban strategic (saturation) use of nuclear weapons against civilian population centers while still using tactical nuclear weapons against military objectives. This is part of the "counterforce" position of the Air Force, which has the heaviest investment in and dependence on nuclear weaponry; it is also the position one identifies with the earlier writings of Henry Kissinger. The other version seeks explicit or implicit agreements to restrict war to the use of conventional weapons—a ban on nuclear weapons altogether. Not too surprisingly, this position has been suggested by the Army, which is less dependent upon nuclear technology.

Both versions of limited war assume that international conflicts can be conducted as gentlemanly affairs in which certain codes of conduct would be adhered to by the military on both sides. It also assumes that adequate, but not survival-state, morale could be generated and maintained in civilian populations. The proponents of limited war see it as a strategy that will enable us to protect the Free World by countering aggression wherever it may occur about the perimeter of our sphere of influence. It would permit us to meet aggression with appropriately graded military response. The use of tactical nuclear weapons would be to the advantage of the United States, it is said, because it substitutes highly mobile and devastating firepower for sheer manpower. Furthermore, the argument goes, being prepared to fight and win limited wars would allow us to take the initiative in foreign policy in traditional ways.

Just how valid are these arguments? In the first place, we can now expect the Russians quickly to cancel our advantage in tactical nuclear weapons with similar devices of their own. Second, as to protecting the Free World, one can see how countries being "protected" might take a very dim view of being the sites of localized devastation. After all, the whole idea of limited war in a nuclear age is to keep conflicts localized *elsewhere* than in the heartlands of the major powers. And what about initiative? Both the Communist bloc and the Free World have had conventional weapons available in large numbers for a long time, but we have witnessed a Great Freeze on initiative rather than the reverse. Nor is there likely to be much initiative along traditional, tension-increasing lines as long as the only protection against full-scale nuclear war is the fear of it.

The fatal flaw in the limited war argument is what experts have come to call *escalation*. However appealing the notion of "gentlemanly war" may be to military men, it hardly seems feasible. The attitudes and emotions generated in wartime by the frustrations of a war economy, by the injury and death of loved ones, and by identification of civilians with far-flung symbols of victory and defeat create an explosive psychological atmosphere. Modern wars are waged by whole populations, not just by a few champions following rigid codes of honor. Victories and defeats are viewed passionately, not with the indifference of peasants watching the war games of mercenaries. The will to sacrifice and fight is a monolithic energy, not easily guided in its course.

Even though a conflict might begin as a localized affair and be waged at first with conventional weapons, reversals in the field would lead to demands for heavier firepower. If tactical nuclear weapons were available, field commanders would be under pressure to employ them; they might be directed against what were conceived by the attacker to be tactical, military targets, but humans are fallible, and what was seen as tactical by one side could easily be viewed as strategic by the other. In the real world, "tactical" and "strategic" do not come in separate geographical packages, but are interspersed and overlapping. When facing a disastrous defeat, full of the hatreds generated by war, people who would normally shun the very thought of nuclear bombing of men, women, and children in the enemy's cities might clamor for it.

There may be a morally and psychologically discernible dividing line between conventional and nuclear weapons—which there is not between tactical and strategic nuclear weapons—but even this line is fine and easily crossed under the exigencies of war. Furthermore, it is clear that as long as strategic nuclear weapons exist, are available and stockpiled, there always exists the possibility of their use. Therefore limited war cannot be said to eliminate the threat to our biological survival—one of the minimal criteria we have established for rational policy. Indeed, it is the presence of massive retaliatory capacity "in the closet" that is supposed to keep limited wars limited. The very horror of full-scale nuclear war is supposed to prevent antagonists from unleashing it. But, by the very same reasoning, this same horror already should have led us to nuclear disarmament, promptly and eagerly agreed to on all sides—but it has not. If the horror of nuclear war has not had this effect in a time of relative peace, what hope can we have that it will serve as a sufficient restraint in time of war?

THE NEANDERTHAL WAY

An ambiguous situation, full of complexities, paradoxes, and dangers that tradition does not handle, is intolerable to the Neanderthal mentality. One response is to deny the whole unpleasant business, and, as we have seen, this leads to passive drift rather than to active, problem-solving manipulation of the situation. Another response is to keep trying to force a traditional mold onto the new situation where it will not fit; the limited war alternative is an example. But the most characteristic Neanderthal response to an ambiguous, threatening situation is to try to burst out of it in a fit of emotion; no doubt archeological rubble heaps are full of cracked, half-finished flint knives and axheads that met this fate.

The longer a deterrent stalemate persists, the greater becomes the internal pressure to escape from the intolerable situation in one way or another. One way of bursting loose is what specialists call *preventive war*. The decision to wage a preventive war is not based on immediate fear of attack from the opponent, but rather on the piled-up anger and frustration of a prolonged cold war. This decision implies a sufficient real or imagined lead in the arms race to make the gamble worth taking. The purpose is to eliminate a source of present frustration and future threat. Another way of bursting loose is what experts now refer to as *pre-emptive war*. The decision in this case does come from fear—fear of imminent surprise attack by the enemy. It does not depend upon real or imagined advantage in the arms race, but rather upon the obvious advantage of a first strike if nuclear war is going to happen.

A preventive war would necessarily begin with a surprise attack that would make Pearl Harbor seem like a tea party in slow motion. Why a surprise attack? Why not a warning threat to do so? Because the whole purpose is to eliminate, as fully and completely as possible, the capacity of the opponent to retaliate— not to frighten him into making his own pre-emptive strike first. This means that preparations for a preventive war must be made in absolute secrecy, and the decision must be reached by other than democratic processes. A totalitarian system would seem to be better able to adopt this alternative. In a democratic country like ours, such a decision would probably mean a military coup, with or without tacit agreement of top leaders in the civilian administration. In considering the likelihood of this alternative, it must be kept in mind that the military advantage need not be real; knowing how beliefs tend to follow desires, it is easy to understand how the military of one side could overestimate their own strength relative to that of the other side. Furthermore, the "lead" need not be in terms of superior weapons or defenses; a cleverly designed infiltration of our hardened bases and submarines would serve just as well, as would a disorganizing "suit-case" attack.

What about the long-term effects of a preventive war? Even though Neanderthal Man seldom looked far beyond his tomor-row, we must do so. In terms of world opinion, whichever nation launches a massive surprise attack becomes the prime source of threat and the chief target for aggression by the rest of the world. The "winner" by such a means would have to maintain constant military readiness, would have to keep the rest of the world cowed by constant threat of nuclear attack, and would almost certainly become isolated—economically, politically, so-cially, and psychologically. Its citizens would have to live, some-how, with the guilt of literally millions of human deaths on their hands and on their minds, and the most likely psychological de-fense against this guilt would be the adoption of complete callous-ness toward human life and values, a gradual descent into a mire of amorality. Is this a future we want? And what would have been "won"? Not the real war with Communism as a way of life; this we would have lost, both at home and abroad.

Pre-emptive war is a much more likely alternative, and its long-term effects are probably much the same. If at some time a nu-clear war appears inevitable, the advantage of striking first is very great. This is particularly true during the present, transition stage, while the retaliatory capacities of both sides are more "soft" than "hard." This means that unless there can be very rapid and full communication between opponents at times of crisis—to dispel what has been called "the reciprocal fear of surprise at-tack"—either side may choose what seems to be the lesser risk of attacking first, convinced that the other side is about to do the same thing. The situations that could produce pre-emption are innumerable: an accidental missile firing, rebellion in a satellite country on either side, playing "chicken" in a crisis situation like Berlin. The cold war mentality fosters the conviction that the enemy, being unlike us in both morality and rationality, *is* likely to strike first in time of crisis. And, of course, this conviction justifies our acting immorally and irrationally first to beat him to the punch. In trying to burst free of intolerable ambiguity, the Neanderthal within us is liable to bring the world down about his own ears.

THE WAY OF THE PACIFIST

There are many people for whom violence in any form between humans is intolerable and for whom the taking of human
lives as a means of resolving conflict is repugnant. Some of these
people, but by no means all, reject violence as a matter of religious principle. Whatever may be their reasons, we call such
people pacifists, and they usually work very hard for peace and
against war. In time of war, be it "hot" or "cold," when nationalistic
fervor is running high, pacifists come to be thought of as weak as
well as passive, and even as bad and dangerous; they become the
target of derogatory terms, like "softheads" and "bleeding hearts."
But pacifists are certainly not evil, nor are they weak and timid;
it takes more courage to stand up for an unpopular cause than it
does to stand up in a mob and growl. Nor are they necessarily
"softheaded"; there would be more rationality in laying down
one's arms in a nuclear age than in using them—if that were the
decision to be made.

My argument with most pacifists concerns the *feasibility* of
their position, not its rationality and certainly not its ultimate
goal. It may be true that complete and abrupt unilateral disarmament by either the United States or Russia would lead eventually to reciprocal disarmament by the other side. And it is entirely possible that in the long run Gandhian passive resistance
would defend and preserve our way of life. But are these things
feasible for societies at the crest of nationalism? I do not think so.
As a matter of fact, any government that announced such a policy
would not have its orders accepted and followed by its military
and certainly would not long stay in power. By urging policies
that are beyond the pale of present acceptability, many pacifists
rule themselves out of the Great Debate and thereby lose their
effectiveness.

However, reactions to the pacifist position do serve to draw
forth and illuminate the deepest resistance to any nonaggressive
alternative. This is *the bogey man conception of the enemy.* To
illustrate this point, let me recall the good philosopher, Socrates,
from his grave and ask him to apply his method of questioning,
first to a Russian man-on-the-street and then to a typical American.

Appearing on the streets of Moscow and falling into stride with

Ivan, Socrates says, "Suppose that American Man were to decide that war under present conditions is intolerable and were to publicly to junk all his weapons. Would you, Russian Man, leap to destroy him in nuclear holocaust?" "Why no," replies Ivan. "We have no desire to destroy people, even the Capitalists. We merely want to be left alone and allowed to live in our own way." Socrates then asks, "Would you overrun the United States and make Communist slaves of the American people? That's what they're afraid of, you know." Ivan stops abruptly. "*We* have no imperialist ambitions," he says, "and in any case, that will take care of itself; Socialism is the wave of the future. All we want to do is live in peace." "All right, then," says the wise Socrates, "do you think American Man would leap to destroy *you* with his nuclear missiles if you were to lay down your weapons?" Ivan stirs the dust with the toe of his boot. "I'm afraid they would," he says finally. "The people in America would have nothing to say about it, and their leaders are warmongers. We must defend ourselves."

Materializing suddenly in John's living room, the good Socrates gives him greeting and seats himself. "Suppose that Russian Man were publicly to junk all of his weapons. Would you, American Man, leap to destroy him in nuclear holocaust?" Recovering from his surprise, John replies, "Of course not. We are only concerned with protecting ourselves, not destroying others." Socrates then asks, "Would you overrun the Soviet Union, once they were helpless, and make Capitalist slaves of the people?" John leans back in his chair, laughing. "For goodness' sake, what a crazy idea! *We* have no imperialist ambitions, and in any case, a world unified under our way of life would be just as good for them as it is for us. To tell the truth," John adds, "we Americans would welcome the chance to get rid of the weapons, the taxes, and all, and live in peace for a change." "All right, then," says the wise Socrates, "do you think that Russian Man would leap to destroy *you* with his nuclear missiles if you were to render yourselves defenseless?" Here there is a long pause. Finally John answers. "Maybe they would and maybe they wouldn't, but we can't take the chance. Didn't Nikita say that he'd bury us? As soon as our guard was down, they'd overrun the whole world, including us, and make Communists out of everybody."

Socrates, the philosopher good and wise, shakes his tousled gray head in puzzlement. How can men so much the same perceive each other as so intrinsically different? Raising his eyes to the heavens, he says: εἴθε μὲν δαίμων τις παρασχοίη ἅπασιν ἡμῖν τὴν δύναμιν τοῦ γνῶναι ἐμαυτοὺς ὡς οἱ ἄλλοι ἡῆς ἔγνωσαν, which, freely translated from the language of ancient Greece, means, "I wish some Power would give us all the gift to see ourselves as others see us!" And, in the way of an afterthought, Socrates continues: εἴθε δὲ ὁ δαίμων οὗτος παρασχοίη ἡμῖν καὶ τὴν δύναμιν τοῦ γνῶναί τοὺς ἄλλους ὡς αὐτοὶ ἑαυτοὺς ἔγνωσαν, which, freely translated, says, "And would that Power also give us the gift to see others as they see themselves!" But this, as Socrates knows only too well, is a great deal to ask of ordinary mortals.

I can almost hear outcries from many readers at this point. All this is fantastically and incredibly unrealistic! It may be true that Americans would treat a defenseless enemy in humane ways —would neither launch an attack on him nor impose a different way of life by force—but the Communists are another matter altogether. Khrushchev *did* say they would bury us. And as Sidney Hook has said, men like Stalin, Bulganin, *and* Khrushchev—the whole crew in the Kremlin—are power-mad fanatics. "Today, a Communist world would be a tightly knit despotism of fear without sanctuaries, without interstices to hide, without possibilities for anonymity. . . . A Communist world could easily become a scientific Gehenna . . . our children and grandchildren may curse us for turning them over to the jailers of a Communist 1984 in which, brainwashed and degraded, they are not even free to die until their masters give them leave."

Now I lay no claim to exclusive possession of the truth, and it may be that Hook is more nearly right in all this than I am. But I can show how such bogey man conceptions of the enemy develop naturally out of the dynamics of human thinking—when little minds seek simple consistencies in a complex world or big minds like Hook's operate under intense emotion. As is usually the case, the truth probably lies somewhere in between both extremes. Our own psycho-logic prevents us from seeing the other fellow objectively and thus keeps us from being able to sift the real differences from the imaginary. The Delphic admonition to "Know thyself" is apropos here; only to the extent that we understand the workings of our own minds can we ever hope to arrive at decisions that are consistent with reason and reality.

In any case, it is clear that here lies the source of greatest resistance to any policies of a conciliatory, nonaggressive nature. Even to question the simple consistency of WE as all white and THEY as all black is to disrupt the basic framework on which the whole world view for most of us is established. It is this primal, unquestioned assumption about the enemy that makes the extreme pacifist position completely infeasible for our time, no matter how morally or rationally satisfying it may be. But the bogey man conception also hamstrings less extreme alternatives. Since a real bogey can be counted on to take advantage of you wherever possible, any compromise on our part must be interpreted as a sign of weakness and any unilateral step designed to reduce tensions must be considered appeasement. As Socrates discovered, however, the Russians have the same view of the world, but in reverse: our whites are their blacks and vice versa. If neither side will back down, mutual bogey man images can lead nowhere other than to mutual annihilation. As difficult as it may be for Homo Sapiens to apply Socrates' Scottish remedy, this is just what we must do if we are to survive.

LET US SIT DOWN AND TALK

The traditional, if seldom successful, way that Homo Sapiens goes about resolving international conflicts other than by war has been through negotiating mutual agreements, pacts, and treaties governing armaments. If such agreements could be achieved, and they included reduction and final elimination of nuclear weapons, there would be no question but what one of our policy criteria—removal of the threat to our biological survival—would be met. Such agreements would also serve to reduce the external threat felt by all parties and thus should create conditions favoring our way of life as against totalitarian ways—another of our prime criteria for policy. But here, as with unilateral disarmament, the problem is *feasibility*.

It is unfortunate but true that the history of disarmament negotiations reveals an inverse relation between urgency and achievement: the greater the need the poorer the prospects. This is because both sides bring to the negotiation table precisely those attitudes and beliefs about the other which generated the arms

race in the first place. Yet success in negotiation requires awareness of the greater threat, a trust in the essential humanity of the
enemy, and hence a willingness to compromise. As Bertrand Russell so wisely (but, I fear, rather naively) said, successful negotiation requires both sides to accept a course in which neither gains
and neither loses. But under conditions of high tension and distrust both sides want to "win" the negotiation and view any compromise as a defeat.

The proposals that have been presented by both the U.S.S.R.
and the United States for general and complete disarmament are
actually quite similar. Both envision the setting up of disarmament machinery within some international body (presumably the
United Nations), this machinery including facilities for inspecting
and verifying that agreed-upon steps have in fact been taken;
both see disarmament moving through several stages of increasing magnitude and significance until complete disarmament is
achieved; both would have amount of inspection increase with
the degree of disarmament. There are differences, to be sure—in
the types of inspection, in the organization and authority of the
international control body, and so forth—but there would seem
to be nothing so serious as to rule out the possibility of successful
negotiation.

Nevertheless, it is clear that neither side has any real hope that
agreements will be reached through negotiation. Why? When
both sides agree on the extraordinary danger created by the existence of nuclear weapons, when both sides express earnest (and,
I believe, sincere) desires for peace, when both sides agree
reasonably well on how to go about it, why are they unable to
get together? What are the mechanisms in human thinking
under conflict conditions that work against successful negotiation?

One is what I have called *biased perception of the equable.*
It is a familiar psychological fact that human perceptions and
meanings are easily influenced by previous conditioning, existing
attitudes, and dominant motives. If the larger of two moving
dots on a screen is shown behind the smaller, it is always "chas-
ing" the little one; but if the larger is shown in front of the smaller,
it is always "leading" the little one—not being chased. Past
experience with interpersonal relations dictates how we perceive

in this new situation. The objectively impassive face of a man in a picket line looks "threatening" to a representative of management but "determined" to a representative of labor—their attitudes toward the man in the picket line differ. Men who have just experienced failure become sensitized to words signifying failure; hungry men are prone to see food objects where there are none. In general, most signs, be they words or perceived things like faces, are potentially ambiguous, and we usually give them interpretations that suit our momentary expectations and purposes. As a person's emotional tension goes up—as he becomes more hungry, more angry, more anxious, as the case may be— his ways of perceiving and interpreting become more rigid and inflexible. This is one reason why the prospects for successful negotiation go down as cold war tensions go up.

Bertrand Russell's rule about both sides accepting a course in which neither wins or loses may be logical, but it is not psychological. What one side perceives as equable (fair, balanced, just) is likely to be perceived by the other as inequable (unfair, unbalanced, unjust). Given their quite different national histories, Russians and Americans approach negotiations with different sets of meaning for the same critical concepts: "inspection" means espionage for one but elimination of secrecy for the other; "the United Nations" means a biased tool for one but an unbiased international body for the other; "overseas bases" means aggressive intent to one but defensive intent to the other—and so on ad infinitum. And even if the actual negotiators at the table are sufficiently sophisticated to avoid these psychological distortions, most of the people at home and the mass media that report to them on the progress of negotiations are not so sophisticated; they impose limitations and restrictions on the degrees of freedom the actual negotiators can display.

There are many *Sacred Cows of policy* that each side imposes on its negotiators. These are points of inflexibility, often given stereotyped labels by the media, on which public opinion is assumed to be so emotionally polarized that representatives in government are afraid to take unpopular positions. These points of assumed inflexibility are often crucial to the success of disarmament negotiations, and I think we ought to determine to what extent the public actually is emotionally polarized and inflexible on them. It is possible for the mass media to create an illusion of unanimity out of the strongly felt opinion of an organized minority. Even if the public is indeed polarized on an issue where flexibility is crucial for successful negotiation, then here is a point where information and education are badly needed. Let us look at a few of the Sacred Cows on our own side of the fence.

One of them is "Nonrecognition of Red China." For years we have been fighting a gradually losing battle to keep Communist China out of the United Nations. Meanwhile we have been supporting Nationalist China—a comparative handful of people displaced to Taiwan (Formosa)—as if it were the legitimate government of the hundreds of millions of Chinese on the mainland. Clearly, the Communist government in Peiping, whether we happen to approve of it or not, does meet all the usual criteria of a stable government, and the rest of the world realizes this (even most of our allies). It is also clear that we cannot have successful disarmament treaties—which, given the nature of nuclear weapons, must be universal—when an aggressive government representing about one-fourth of the population of the globe is not included. Reason says that the best way to handle Red China is to include it within the community of nations and to work gradually for its acceptance of common rules of international behavior. To continue to isolate the Chinese Communists means to give them even more justification for aggression when they do break loose and when they do acquire nuclear weapons. But emotion dictates otherwise.

Another Sacred Cow is "a Unified Germany." One searches the history of conferences and negotiations on Germany in vain for any clear-cut and agreed-upon statement of our rights in Berlin. A jointly controlled and divided city nearly 200 miles inside the East German border is now, and always was, an unstable and untenable situation. It is also clear that a unified Germany would be acceptable to the Soviets only if both halves were neutralized (and preferably communized). But we see this as the end of NATO and the beginning of communization of all Europe. The Soviets, on the other hand, see a Germany unified and still in NATO as a real bogey man; after all, they did lose almost 20 million lives at the hands of the Germans in the last war. I, for one, must confess that the idea of a reunified Germany (either communized or capitalized) is not entirely appealing. A twice-defeated nation, West Germany has already recovered to the point where it is the economic leader of the Common Market in Europe and militarily the strongest European contributor to NATO. A solution that securely neutralizes both Germanies and eliminates Berlin as a source of repeated crises (perhaps by making it an international city) seems reasonable—but again, emotion dictates otherwise.

Yet another Sacred Cow is the idea that we must always "Negotiate from Strength." By this is meant that we must be militarily, politically, and even psychologically stronger than the opponent before we will negotiate an issue. This view stems from the notion that negotiations are a kind of conflict in which one expects either to win or lose, and if one is not leading from a position of relative strength the point of compromise is more likely to be in the other fellow's favor. But when both parties hold this same Cow to be Sacred—and it is clear that the Russians share this view (they would not negotiate at all on nuclear control and disarmament when they were far behind in this sphere)—it is obvious that nothing can be accomplished. The Russians will not cooperate when they feel weaker and we will not cooperate when we feel weaker. Stalemate. I believe that a careful analysis of past negotiations would cast doubt on the basic assumption here—that points of compromise always favor the stronger party. Often, I suspect, the stronger side is the one more willing to be magnanimous and compromising. We were willing to internationalize nuclear power and weaponry when we were the exclusive possessors; certainly the Japanese and the Germans gained more in the surrender negotiations (even though surrender was unconditional in both cases) than they had any reason to expect.

My last Sacred Cow has been particularly damaging to recent disarmament negotiations; it is the demand for "Foolproof Inspection." Our own negotiators have reached the point where they cannot use the word "disarmament" without quickly adding "with adequate inspection." Since it is technically impossible to achieve foolproof inspection, and "adequate" is a fluid term, many on our side argue that any disarmament is too dangerous. And our most recent demand—for inspection that would disclose *preparations* for testing as well as actual explosions—seems to put agreement beyond possible reach.

Of course the Russians have Sacred Cows on their side of the fence, too. With a closed society's characteristic fear of espionage, they have kept insisting that agreement on general and complete disarmament precede any discussion of inspection (while we, with an open society's characteristic fear of secrecy, have kept insisting on agreement on inspection safeguards prior to any talk about general and complete disarmament). They have also added the "troika" idea: the international control body should be topped by three heads, one from the Communist bloc, one from the Western bloc, and one from the neutrals, and these three heads must be unanimous about the need for specific inspections. Since, to the West, this obviously means a Communist veto whenever they do not wish to be inspected, it has been absolutely unacceptable.

I want to attack the Sacred Cow of foolproof inspection by suggesting some propositions about human behavior and drawing some deductions from them. First, I submit that the felt need for inspection will go down as the degree of mutual trust goes up. We do not feel any need to inspect Canada for concealed missiles or production sites. Why? Because we trust the Canadians. Second, I submit that mutual trust will increase with the degree of disarmament achieved. Most disarmament schemes assume that distrust remains constant despite disarmament; therefore the magnitude and penetration of inspection is made to increase with the degree of disarmament. (The subtle argument here is that the more complete the level of disarmament, the greater the advantage even a few nuclear weapons could give one side; therefore, when complete disarmament has been achieved, legions of international inspectors must be continually crawling over the disarmed nations to make sure they are really that way.) Finally, I submit that the less the mutual trust the more inspection will be perceived as espionage by either side. As long as the Russians suspect surprise attack and see secrecy as a primary defense, they will not permit close inspection. On our own part, we do not restrict the movements of Canadian nationals in our country the way we do the movements of nationals from Communist countries.

From these propositions a number of deductions flow. One is that the objective of felt security can be achieved *either* by increasing mutual inspection *or* by increasing mutual trust. So far we have been working only on techniques of inspection; we would be wise to start working on techniques of building mutual trust. And since the likelihood of achieving successful disarmament negotiations also depends upon the level of mutual trust, as we have already seen, it behooves us to start operating on the atmosphere of distrust before we become completely bogged down on the technicalities of inspection. Last, we can deduce that the type of inspection, and hence the type of enforceable disarmament, must be made to vary flexibly with the level of mutual trust. Rather than requiring maximum inspection, a completely disarmed (and trustful) world would require no more inspection than New York demands of Massachusetts. It is in the early stages, when mutual suspicions are high, that we need careful inspection—and therefore we need to begin with those kinds of disarmament for which internal inspection can be minimal and compliance is easily verified. When we reach the stage where intensive internal inspection is necessary to prove compliance, we will discover that we no longer feel such need for it. The reason this sounds like heresy is that it is being looked at from the standpoint of present levels of distrust and suspicion.

Another major mental dynamic that works against successful negotiations is *the self-fulfilling prophecy*. Each side approaches the negotiations with the conviction that the other will prove unreasonable, stubborn, and completely self-seeking. Before each conference begins, the press in each nation warns its readers that the other side really does not want peace and that therefore they can expect no real progress. Each side believes that the other is really using the negotiations to gain a victory on the cold war propaganda front—which, of course, they both are, because they expect nothing else to be accomplished. Believing these things, each side behaves during the negotiations so as to "win" in the competition, little or nothing is actually accomplished, and both sides go back home saying, "I told you so!" The prophecy has been fulfilled and the stage has been set for the next prophecy about the next negotiation attempt.

The cold war mentality contributes yet another psychological block to successful negotiations—*distrust in agreements*. One hears it said that treaties with THEM are not worth the paper they are written on. Enemies, by the definition of psycho-logic, are evil, and evil men must be expected to cheat where we would not. Traditionally, one of the deepest American anxieties is about being "taken advantage of," "hornswoggled," and "hoodwinked." Since no inspection system is ever going to be 100 per cent foolproof, there must always remain the possibility of cheating— which again emphasizes the fact that mutual trust is essential. We need to create an international atmosphere in which there is little need or incentive to cheat. But we do not have that kind of atmosphere now, and as long as the prospective signatories have no faith that the other side will abide by agreements, we cannot expect them to negotiate in earnest. Even if the negotiators did negotiate in earnest and achieved significant agreements, it is by no means certain that the agreements would be kept in time of crisis by either side or that they would even be ratified by the United States Senate—which would have a disastrous impact upon future international relations. It is clear that we need to develop and apply techniques of controlling tensions and creating mutual trust if disarmament agreements are going to be kept, to say nothing of reached.

An example of this type of psycho-logic appeared in "A Second Open Letter to the Presidential Candidates," written by Thomas E. Murray, ex-chairman of the AEC, and released Friday, November 4, 1960. In this letter he argued for the resumption of testing nuclear weapons by the United States, particularly of a new, "third generation" nuclear weapon, the neutron bomb, which is primarily antipersonnel in nature. (And this in itself is an interesting bit of grist for the mill of those concerned with the human side of policy in a nuclear age; there is great enthusiasm in some quarters for a bomb that will kill more people but destroy less valuable property!) In this letter Murray said, "Nuclear technology does not stand still or stand pat, certainly not in the Soviet Union, which restlessly and in all secrecy seeks the means of military advantage." And later, "I take it for granted that the Soviet Union is actively developing nuclear technology along this revolutionary line. I must assume that they have done some preliminary tests of the new 'fantastic' weapon. Such tests could easily have been carried on without detection." In other words, there was no hard evidence that the Russians were cheating on their self-imposed testing ban, but we must "take it for granted" that they were.

Now there are many who take the fact that the Russians were the first to break the test ban as prima facie evidence that they had been cheating all the time. I would conclude just the reverse; from the public announcement of the breaking of the ban and the rushed flurry of tests following announcement, it would appear that they had not been testing previously but obviously were preparing to do so. Were their preparations for testing a breach of ethics? Yes, but if so, then both sides were equally unethical in this respect; we began underground testing soon afterward, with devices and in sites that obviously required extensive prior preparation. And just before the Soviets broke the test ban, there were press releases here saying that we were about to resume testing if the Russians did not soon reach formal agreements for a test ban with adequate inspection.

None of this is said to justify the Soviet decision to resume testing. It was a dangerous decision—one that threw the arms race back into high gear and that filled our skies with radioactive fallout, the effects of which we will all be living with for some time to come. Why did they make this decision? I suspect that their motives were very much what ours would have been in similar circumstances: increasing tension over Berlin and their fear of a West Germany armed with nuclear weapons, their correct belief that they were behind in a sheer military sense, both in terms of numbers of stockpiled weapons and their efficiency, and their own internal pressures from Stalinists and the Red Chinese for a "get tough" line toward the West. Whatever may have been the combination of reasons, the resumption of nuclear testing by the Soviets confirmed the bogey man image most Americans already had of them and therefore made the path toward a peaceful world all the more rocky. But there is something we should learn from our own reactions to this incident: rather than being frightened into submission and compliance by this show of strength on the part of the Soviets, we have made just the reverse response—a "get even tougher" reaction. We can expect the Soviets to respond similarly to threatening gestures on our part.

We have behind us a long and dismal history of unsuccessful negotiations with the Soviets. It is easy to blame all the difficulty on the Communists, as they blame it all on us, but whatever the final judgment of history may be, it is certain that the same kind of mechanisms operate on both sides. Judging from the woefully inadequate technical preparations of negotiators, and also from the almost complete lack of government support for the study of nonaggressive solutions, it would appear that neither side really holds much hope for reaching agreements on disarmament. Yet the people on both sides earnestly desire peace.

The conclusion we seem driven to is this: *Negotiated agreements require commitments from both sides prior to any action by either, and under the conditions of cold war thinking commitments of any significance seem most unlikely; as long as both sides remain chained to the requirement of prior commitment from the other, neither is able to take the initiative in moving toward a more peaceful world.*

So here we stand with terrible power but shorn of initiative. No one dares to move too abruptly or violently for fear of upsetting the "atom cart." Nuclear technology has rendered the whole conception of winning a war as a means of resolving international conflict anachronistic. Yet we cannot get rid of these fantastic new weapons and go back to the almost friendly pattern of "war as usual"; the knowledge that yields the weapons is here to stay, barring complete destruction of our civilization. We find the unleashing of a preventive or pre-emptive war as morally repugnant as submitting to a Communist way of life. Yet we seem unable to achieve successful agreements with the Russians on disarmament; the same tensions and distrusts that drive the arms race also have seats at the negotiating table. Clearly, some fresh approach is needed if we are to break out of this impasse.

GRIT

5

I believe there is a way out of the dilemma of being either Red or Dead. It is not merely drifting along doing what comes naturally until fate decides the issue for us. It is not trying to erect stabilized deterrence on the shifting sands of human fallibility and hoping that it will somehow last forever. It is neither getting it all over with in an angry burst of hell-fire nor passively hoping for the best from an aggressive opponent as we lay down our arms. It is not merely keeping up the effort to reach negotiated agreements with the enemy, although such efforts should be continued. The way out, I think, lies in an approach quite novel for competing sovereign states: taking the initiative, not by creating threats and tensions but by reducing and controlling them.

In this chapter I want you to join me in exploring the possibilities that may lie in unilateral initiative of a particular kind. The technical term for this policy is *Graduated Reciprocation in Tension-reduction*. This mouth-filling phrase was the title of a paper of mine in which I first elaborated the nature of this approach to international relations.[1] It says exactly what I want to say, as you will see, but I soon discovered that no one could correctly remember it. I also discovered—while doodling and making notes at a conference one day—that the initials of this technical term spell GRIT. This was a happy, if entirely unintentional, discovery. GRIT is not only something everyone can remember, it also suggests the kind of national determination that will be required if we are to escape from being either Red or Dead.

THE ARMS RACE IN REVERSE

John and Ivan stand facing each other near the middle, but on opposite sides, of a long, rigid, neatly balanced seesaw. This seesaw is balanced on a point that juts out over a bottomless abyss. As either of these two husky men takes a step outward on his side away from the center, the other must quickly compensate with an equal step outward on his side, or the balance will be destroyed. The farther out they move, the greater the unbalancing effect of each unilateral step, and the more agile and quick to react both John and Ivan must be to keep the precarious equilibrium.

To make the situation even worse, both of these men realize full well that this teetering board must have some limit to its tensile strength; sooner or later, if they keep moving out against each other, it is bound to crack, dropping them both down to destruction. So both John and Ivan are frightened. Yet neither is willing to admit his own fear because his opponent might take advantage of him.

How are these two men to escape from this dangerous situation—a situation in which the fate of each is bound up with that of the other? One reasonable solution immediately presents itself. Let both of them agree to walk slowly and carefully back toward the center of the teetering board in unison. To reach such an agreement they must trust each other. But the whole trouble is that these two husky men do *not* trust each other; each believes the other to be irrational enough to destroy them both unless he himself preserves the balance.

---

[1] Subsequently published in a collection called *The Liberal Papers*, by Doubleday (Anchor Book 290), 1962, but with the title "Reciprocal Initiative."

But now let us suppose that, during a quiet period in their strife, it occurs to one of these men that perhaps the other is really just as frightened as he himself is. If this were so, he would also welcome some way of escaping from this intolerable situation. So this man decides to gamble a little on his new insight. Loudly he calls out, "I am taking a small step *toward* you when I count to ten!" The other man, rather than risk having the precious balance upset, also takes a small, tentative step forward at the count of ten. Whereupon the first announces another larger step forward, and they both take it as the count is made. Thus John and Ivan gradually work their ways back to safety by a series of self-initiated, but reciprocated, steps—very much as they had originally moved out against each other.

This little parable contains the essential idea of GRIT. It is simply this—that the tensions/arms race spiral may offer the model for its own reversal. As a type of international behavior, just what is an arms race? *An arms race is a kind of graduated and reciprocated, unilaterally initiated, internation action.* Is it unilaterally initiated? A nation developing a new weapon, increasing its stockpile of nuclear warheads, or setting up a new military base certainly does not wait for any prior agreement with the opponent. Is it reciprocal? Each increase in military power by one side provides the threat stimulus for the other to try to catch up and get ahead. Is it graduated? Necessarily—first by the irregular and somewhat unpredictable nature of technological breakthroughs and second by the oscillating nature of the threat stimulus itself.

But an arms race is obviously a *tension-increasing* system; it is a spiral of terror. By reversing one of the characteristics of an arms race, we may be able to transform it into a spiral of trust. This would be a graduated and reciprocated, unilaterally initiated, internation system that was *tension-decreasing* in nature. This is entirely conceivable, you may say, but the real question is this: is it *feasible* under present conditions of national sovereignty, of mutual fear and distrust? I will try to show that, with anything like the dedication and energy now being thrown into the arms race, GRIT would be feasible. This does not mean that it would be easy. There is no magically simple formula for peace.

Before plunging into the details of this plan, we should get an overview of its nature and purpose. GRIT must be sharply distinguished from the kind of abrupt and complete disarmament sponsored by many pacifist groups. To the contrary, what I am proposing is a flexible, self-regulating procedure in which the participants carefully monitor their own initiatives on the basis of their own evaluation of the reciprocating actions taken by the other side. It is broader than disarmament, or even disengagement as this is usually conceived, since it would include programs of graded initiatives of a tension-reducing nature in areas of science and secrecy, of economic, social, and cultural exchanges, of Communist China and the United Nations, of controls and inspections, of diplomatic adjustments, and so forth—as well as actual military and disarmament steps.

It could be viewed as a "peace offensive." In a way, it is an application of the Golden Rule on an international scale—but a Golden Rule with built-in safeguards. It is perhaps best viewed as a kind of international (rather than interpersonal) communicating and learning situation, where the communication is more by deeds than by words and where what is learned—hopefully and gradually—is increased mutual understanding and trust.

What are the aims of GRIT? One is *to reduce and control international tension levels.* The intimate relation we have found between tension and both irrationality in human decision-making and instability of the military environment puts a high premium on devising and applying techniques of tension control. Another aim is *to create gradually an atmosphere of mutual trust within which negotiations on critical political and military issues will have a better chance of succeeding.* Significant agreements are almost impossible when mutual fears and suspicions are running high. Yet another aim of GRIT is *to enable this country to take the initiative in foreign policy.* We have been passively defending the status quo too long, and nuclear weaponry has further frozen initiative along traditional lines; there is much to be done in the real war with Communism, and it is high time we were about it. A final aim I will mention is *to launch a new kind of international behavior that is appropriate to the nuclear age.* Traditional forms of international relations have been outmoded by our technology, and our sociopolitical machinery must catch up if we are to survive.

However, being unconventional in nature—and worse, being conciliatory—GRIT is open to suspicion abroad and resistance at home, particularly under the conditions of the cold war mentality. Therefore it needs to be spelled out in detail and critically evaluated. We need to demonstrate that it is possible for a nation to take the initiative in reducing tensions, and yet operate within reasonable limits of national dignity and security. Specifically, it is necessary to indicate the characteristics the unilateral initiatives in such a program must have in order to maintain adequate felt security while at the same time inducing reciprocative behavior from an opponent. Furthermore, we will want to provide some guidelines for selecting our initiatives, in terms of the goals we wish to accomplish. And we must say something about how the genuineness and significance of our initiations and their reciprocations can be evaluated. In other words, while admittedly idealistic in purpose and aiming toward the same ultimate goal as the most adamant pacifist, GRIT must be shown to be realistic and feasible within the existing military, political, economic, and psychological situation.

MAINTAINING NATIONAL SECURITY

Maintaining security means more than avoiding military defeats, more than protecting and keeping what belongs to us, and even more than preventing nuclear suicide. It also means strengthening the institutions that keep us free at home and supporting the freedoms of others to choose the institutions under which they will live. The notion of "national security" thus includes two of the prime criteria of policy we established in an earlier chapter: biological survival and preserving our way of life. The unilateral initiatives that give substance to Graduated Reciprocation in Tension-reduction must be shown to satisfy reasonable requirements of national security, while at the same time risking enough of it in small bits to induce reciprocation from opponents and thereby reduce world tensions. Impossible, you say? We shall see.

(a) *Unilateral initiatives must not reduce our capacity to inflict unacceptable nuclear retaliation on an opponent should we be attacked.*

I would be the first to agree that nuclear deterrence does not provide any real security in the long run, and GRIT is designed to create conditions under which nuclear weapons could eventually be eliminated. But, on the other hand, both the United States and the Soviet Union are moving as rapidly as they can toward what strategists call "stabilized deterrence," a situation in which both sides have highly invulnerable second-strike (retaliatory) nuclear capabilities. These may consist of "hardened" land bases, mobile, nuclear-powered submarines armed with Polaris-type missiles, or even some fantastic weapons systems not dreamed of as yet. Given present levels of tension, it is not likely that these ultimate weapons will be given up. This is an unpleasant fact about life in the dawn of the nuclear age, and we must deal with it if our policy is to meet the criterion of feasibility.

Nuclear retaliatory capacity can serve rational foreign policy (1) *if it is viewed not only as a deterrent but also as a security base from which to take limited risks in the direction of reducing tensions.* This is a very important point. The capacity to carry certain and completely unacceptable nuclear destruction to an opponent obviously is a means of deterring him from launching an attack—as long as he behaves rationally. But except for first-strike possibilities, this has been the *only* function given this capacity by military and political strategists. The same capacity can also function as a base for security. Since the enemy knows that we can literally wipe him off the face of the map if he attacks or otherwise tries to take advantage of us (and we know the same about his capacity), both sides are able to take limited risks, secure in the knowledge that the opponent will be cautious. This applies to limited risk in tension-induction (as has been going on in Berlin), but it also applies to limited risk in tension-reduction—and only the latter offers long-run security.

Nuclear retaliatory capacity can serve rational foreign policy (2) *if the retaliatory or second-strike nature of the capacity is made explicit.* Now it is true that militarily it is difficult to distinguish cleanly between first- and second-strike weapons. The missiles on a Polaris submarine could be used for a surprise attack as well as for retaliation. On the other hand, it is also true that technological and political, as well as psychological, steps can be taken to emphasize the second-strike possibility and de-emphasize the first-strike possibility. Technologically, anything that makes missile sites less vulnerable to attack emphasizes second-strike use, because we are better able to delay and weigh decisions without seriously weakening our retaliatory capacity. Hence the urge to pre-empt becomes less. Politically, we can accept a moral prohibition against the first use of nuclear weapons. Some elements of the military establishment resist such political inhibition, on the ground that it reduces their freedom of choice in responding to aggression, but reducing freedom of choice by the military is a necessary ingredient of arms control and tension control. Psychologically, we can cease and desist from "rocket rattling" as a tactic in the cold war. This tactic does not increase the credibility of our *retaliatory* capacity, since the enemy knows full well we will use it if attacked.

Nuclear retaliatory capacity can serve rational foreign policy (3) *if the minimum capacity required for effective deterrence is maintained and the arms race discontinued.* What is the distinction between an "arms race mentality" and a "deterrence philosophy"? The arms race mentality takes it for granted that we must keep ahead of the opponent in total military power in order to be secure; it assumes that if some new weapon can be devised, then the enemy (who is always seeking the advantage) will develop it, and therefore so must we; it also assumes that the credibility of our deterrence increases directly with the sheer power and number of our weapons. The essence of a deterrence philosophy is that there is some maximum degree of destruction that the opponent can rationally tolerate (and if he is irrational, he is not going to be deterred anyhow); therefore, there must be some limited capacity for nuclear retaliation which will be sufficient to deter him. The following figure contrasts the "arms race mentality" with the "deterrence philosophy." The deterrence logic (curved line) says that to be able to annihilate an opponent once deters him almost as much as to be able to annihilate him 10 or even 1,000 times over—and we are interested in deterrence, not annihilation.

The approach to disarmament implicit in GRIT is to give up nuclear deterrents last. This is a somewhat novel approach and quite the opposite of most disarmament proposals, which ask for nuclear disarmament first and popguns last. The usual approach has emotional appeal because it seeks to get rid of the weapons we fear most first, but I do not think it is rational. As long as

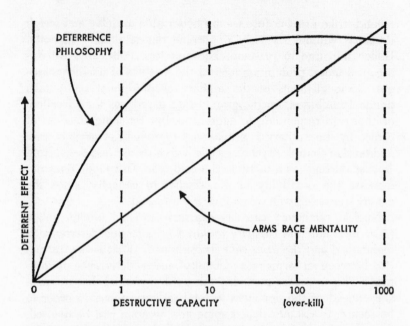

nationalistic tensions and technical know-how exist, popguns can start conflicts that end up in nuclear holocaust. Furthermore, since nuclear weapons represent so much destructive capacity in such little packages, their existence is harder to inspect and control than is the massing and movement of conventional forces and weapons. I think that we must retain the minimum nuclear retaliatory capacity necessary for deterrence, *and* for security in limited risk-taking, until international tensions have been reduced—reduced to a point where final elimination of the nuclear safeguards themselves can be achieved by successfully negotiated treaties.

(b) *Unilateral initiatives must not cripple our capacity to meet aggression by conventional weapons with appropriately graded conventional military responses.*

One of the main sources of resistance to nuclear disarmament comes from those who believe that if we were to remove this threat, the Communists would continue to nibble away at the Free World by other means until we were isolated. Actually, it is debatable whether our possession of nuclear weapons over a decade or more has done much to help us in the real war against Communism around the world. This, of course, is the reason for recent emphasis upon strengthening our conventional capabilities. Unilateral initiatives on our part should not serve to weaken such capacity for conventional military operations directly, *but should create conditions in which the magnitude of such capability could be gradually reduced as part of the total policy.*

There are two main ways in which conventional forces and armaments can be reduced by GRIT. One is by direct initiative —that is, by using small steps in conventional disarmament, disengagement, or arms control as a means of reducing tensions. To the extent that these steps are reciprocated, our capacity to meet remaining sources of aggression by appropriately graded conventional response stays relatively the same—has not been "degraded," as the military phrase goes. The other is by transfer of conventional forces and armaments to an international police force under United Nations or similar auspices. This transfer of conventional capacity to the United Nations to counter aggression can be accomplished either by unilateral initiative (presumably, but not necessarily, with reciprocation) or by negotiated agreements. Both Soviet and United States disarmament proposals include phased transfer of conventional weapons to an international peace-keeping machinery.

At this point, no doubt, the Voice of the Dove is asking, "How can you say you are trying to reduce international tensions when you insist that we retain both our nuclear and our conventional armaments?" In the first place, this is not exactly what I have been saying; rather, I have argued that we should retain only the minimum nuclear capacity required for sufficient deterrence (and this only temporarily) and that we should gradually reduce our conventional forces by reciprocated initiatives and by transfer to the United Nations. In the second place, I would argue that there is no simple and direct relation between tensions and armaments; it is possible to modify the threat significance of armaments by a wide variety of actions that in themselves do not constitute disarmament. Then, in a less tense atmosphere, it should become easier to deal with armaments per se. And in the third place, I believe it would be disastrous from anyone's point of view— pacifist or otherwise—to take initiatives early in the game that would either openly invite aggression abroad or create extreme anxiety at home. We must begin by working within the requirements of the existing situation, even though we have the aim of gradually changing it. This is why we should not reduce our conventional forces abruptly and why we should not initiate actions that might endanger our "heartland." If taken advantage of, we might release full-scale nuclear retaliation and thereby write "finis" to this chapter of the human book.

(c) *Unilateral initiatives must be graduated in risk according to the degree of reciprocation obtained from opponents.*

This is the essential self-regulating characteristic of GRIT. It is the characteristic that makes it possible for us to keep within tolerable limits of total national security while continuing to apply pressure on an opponent to join our march toward peace. The size of the step taken at any particular time—the amount of security we are risking should reciprocation not be obtained or even should our step be taken advantage of—depends upon our own evaluation of what the other side has been doing up to that point in response to previous initiatives. If the Soviets had shown no signs of reciprocating, or had been offering what seemed to be only token reciprocations, we would keep right on moving, but with further small-risk initiatives. If, on the other hand, they had taken some verifiably significant, tension-reducing steps of their own, we would be in a position to increase the significance of our own next actions. The process can be slowed down or speeded up as the conditions of the moment require, but it should be kept going.

Another basis for graduation of action is the stage of the program in each sphere and locus (see the next section). In general, earlier initiatives in each program would be smaller in magnitude of risk potential than later initiatives in the same program. For example, in the political sphere of the Red China locus we would invite diplomatic exchanges before we joined in moving the substitution of Red China for Nationalist China on the Security Council of the United Nations (assuming Red China had already been seated in the General Assembly). Furthermore, the early steps in each sphere and locus would be designed to facilitate later steps in the same program. This indicates the intimate relation between maintaining security and inducing reciprocation.

In a sense, the *relative* risk potential of our initiatives in any program would remain roughly constant; this is because clear reciprocation by an opponent of an earlier step makes it possible for us to take a larger step with no greater real risk than another small step would have meant before.

(d) *Unilateral initiatives must be diversified in nature, both as to sphere of action and as to geographical locus of application.*

By "sphere of action" here is meant the substance of the initiative—whether cultural, scientific, economic, political, legal, disarmament, military, or so on. The range of opportunities here is as broad as all the ways in which actions by one country can have impact on the interest and well-being of another. It is clearly not limited to disarmament or military moves. The only thing that binds the diversified initiatives in GRIT together is their explicit intent to reduce and control tensions on our part—and, hopefully, their tension-reducing impact upon others. Sharing information about health and providing medical aid when it is urgently needed can have just as much psychological impact upon international tensions as actual reduction in armaments.

By "geographical locus" is meant the nation or nations primarily affected by our initiatives and involved in the reciprocating process. The locus of action may be, and often will be, nations we perceive as opponents (Russia, Communist China, the entire Communist bloc, Cuba), but it may also be a neutral nation (India, Yugoslavia, the Congo, Finland), or it may be within our own bloc (West Germany, the Common Market, Latin America, Japan). Of course, certain initiatives may be aimed at, and invite reciprocation from, all nations. As a kind of international behavior, GRIT can be applied to reducing and controlling tensions between "friendly" countries as well as "unfriendly" (that is, within blocs as well as between them), it can be applied to economic conflicts as well as political, and it can be applied to small-scale problems as well as large-scale. As a matter of fact, I am told that Graduated Reciprocation in Tension-reduction is commonly used in an informal way to ease the path to successful labor-management negotiations, particularly when tensions are so high that representatives cannot even sit together at the table. And when you think about it, there would be very few successful marriages if husbands and wives did not practice GRIT as a means of resolving family conflicts!

One purpose in diversifying our unilateral initiatives is *to give us maximum flexibility of approach*. When graded programs of actions have been prepared for many different spheres and loci, we have available a large supply of possible initiatives from which to choose. If some particular geographical locus becomes a crisis area (like Berlin, Laos, or the Congo), and we feel it is necessary to remain firm and unyielding at this point, we still are able to keep moving elsewhere across the board with our determined policy of tension-reduction and control—by selecting and executing actions "on schedule" in other loci. If conditions of the moment make it unwise to make further moves in one sphere (for example, in disarmament), we can still keep moving, still keep applying the pressure toward reciprocation, in other spheres. This is the kind of flexibility we must have and use if we are to shift the arms race into reverse.

Another purpose of diversity in our unilateral initiatives is *to make it possible to keep the policy moving without weakening ourselves progressively in any one sphere or locus*. This applies particularly to the critical military and disarmament spheres. If the only way we were able to keep up pressure were to continue taking steps in disarmament or in disengagement—and no reciprocation had been forthcoming from the opponent—even though the individual steps were small, their security risk potentials would cumulate and we would soon find ourselves in a dangerous situation. Similarly with respect to the locus of application, if all of our moves had to be confined to Berlin and Central Europe, we might soon find ourselves in a very unbalanced situation with respect to what was happening in the rest of the world. The availability of possible actions in many different spheres and loci, these actions varying over the spectrum of risk potential, gives us the capacity to maintain balance on a worldwide scale while we pursue the basic policy of GRIT.

(e) *Prior to announcement, unilateral initiatives must be unpredictable by an opponent as to their sphere, locus, and time of execution.*

If an opponent knows ahead of time where we are planning to act and what we are planning to do, he is in a better position to counter our intention by some action of his own, confuse our strategy, and generally weaken the effectiveness of our policy. He may try by propaganda means to distort our intent and influence the interpretation of our action when it comes. Knowing what we plan to do, he may actually try to usurp or encroach in that area so as to transform what would have been a tension-reducing initiative on our part into a tension-increasing bit of aggression on his part. Of course, such "taking advantage of us" would be much more likely in the early stages of GRIT, when distrust and suspicion are high, than in later stages. In order to minimize the likelihood of encroachment, as well as to influence world interpretation and opinion should it happen, our announcements of initiatives should include explicit warnings that we will firmly resist any attempt to take advantage of our intention prior to its execution. In any case, I submit that psychologically an opponent is much less likely to encroach aggressively in an area *after* public announcement of our intent than prior to such announcement, and if he does, he is certainly less likely to gain the support of world public opinion.

However, if encroachments do occur despite our prior announcements of intent and warnings—perhaps to probe the possibility that we are "going soft"—then they must be resisted just as firmly as if this policy were not in operation. Yet this resistance should be explicitly pinpointed to the area of encroachment, designed to restore the status quo there, and not used as an excuse to reverse our policy and risk escalation from limited to general war. Meanwhile, our program of tension-reducing moves should be continued flexibly across the board in other areas. This is clearly a different approach to international relations than the traditional, monolithic reaction of a nation to tension-increasing events, but it is a necessary approach if we are to survive in a nuclear age.

It might be a good thing if attempted encroachments did occur early in the execution of this policy. Why? Because we are involved in the *learning* of a new kind of international behavior, and in learning it is useful to have occasional negative trials in which the wrong behavior can be punished. Something important would be learned by both sides: the opponent would learn that GRIT does not mean "surrender" and the Neanderthal-minded on our own side would learn that it does not mean "appeasement." Under conditions of nuclear deterrence, we can be sure that any encroachments would be tentative and probing in nature, not all-out attacks. Being such, they would provide opportunities for mutual learning rather than invitations to mutual suicide—if they were handled with firmness and self-restraint.

INDUCING RECIPROCATION

Is it possible to maintain adequate national security and at the same time behave in such a way internationally as to induce our opponents to join in a steady march toward peace? Can we retain a nuclear capability sufficient to deter, maintain conventional forces sufficient to meet localized aggression with graded response, resist possible encroachments on our good intentions with pinpointed force—and still expect our opponents to reciprocate? Part of the answer, as we have seen, lies in intelligent arms management, like adopting a deterrence philosophy rather than an arms race mentality and making the retaliatory nature of our nuclear force explicit; part of it lies in the gradual transfer of conventional forces to an international authority like the United Nations; part of it lies in the graduation and diversification of the tension-reducing steps. But the major factor determining the success or failure of GRIT will be the sophistication with which we utilize what we know about human nature in the execution of the policy. Here is the point where all that the behavioral and social sciences can tell us must be brought to bear—and being comparatively youthful sciences, it is not as much as we would like.

(f) *Unilateral initiatives must represent a sincere intent to reduce and control international tensions.*

Is it not perfectly obvious that this would be their intent? Not at all. Certainly, in the beginning, our opponents would not perceive this as the bona fide intent; it is not consistent with the image of us their psycho-logic requires. It is also certain that many on our own side, equally convinced of the validity of their own psycho-logic, would see no hope whatsoever for inducing honest reciprocation from our opponents and therefore would view our initiatives merely as ploys in the cold war. The great danger is that GRIT would become the handmaiden of traditional international power politics, would be used merely as a propaganda tactic to influence world opinion in our favor. We want to influence world opinion in our favor and ultimately win the real war with Communism as a way of life, but we want to do it by achieving a reasonably peaceful world in which the danger of nuclear war is eliminated.

The main point is that we cannot achieve our goals with a patchwork, opportunistic policy in which tradition dominates and new elements are applied only occasionally like actors' paint. We have to rethink completely our policy position in the new world that the nuclear age has given us, decide what our long-run objectives are and where our long-term security lies, and then behave accordingly and consistently. If we do not—if we are really *not* sincere—then this will soon become apparent to both allies and enemies alike; our unilateral initiatives will be reacted to on these terms, and nothing will be accomplished but an intensification of the cold war. Furthermore, when we finally discover that traditional policies will not and can not work in the nuclear age, we may find that this alternative is no longer available to us— we will have "cried wolf" once too often.

If GRIT is to succeed, it must be entered into completely and sincerely, and thereby disentangled from the cold war. If, despite our best and prolonged efforts, reciprocation is not obtained, and therefore the policy fails, the nature of GRIT is such that we will still retain adequate national security and will be very little worse off than we are now. At least we will have given our opponent every reasonable opportunity to demonstrate the sincerity of his desire to escape from the dangerous situation we are both in and together secure a more peaceful world.

(g) *Unilateral initiatives must be announced publicly at some reasonable interval prior to their execution and identified as part of a deliberate policy of reducing and controlling tensions.*

Announcement prior to execution is suggested for several reasons. For one thing, the interval between announcement of a particular action and its completed execution is a period during which pressures toward reciprocation can be expected to grow, both internally and externally. For another thing, the same period provides time for the opponent to evaluate the significance of our action, to weigh carefully the advantages in reciprocating or not reciprocating, and to consider various possible reciprocations and how they should be expressed. Third, announcement in advance of execution would tend to prevent the unstabilizing effect that unexpected, surprise moves might have. True, one might argue that surprising the opponent with sudden, unpredictable events might keep him off base and give us the advantage—but advantage in what sense? Is it to our advantage to keep an opponent who has nuclear weapons in his hands off balance and on edge? Finally, and perhaps most important, prior announcement permits us to influence the opponent's interpretation of our actions when they come. Actions, like words (only less so), are potentially ambiguous and open to various interpretations; by prior announcement and clarification we help to reduce the range of interpretation and emphasize that which we intend.

Of course the time intervals introduced between announcements and executions will vary with the nature of the initiatives. Some actions could be executed soon after announcement of intent—for example, the elimination of trade barriers with Red China. Other actions would require longer intervals—for example, the dismantling of an overseas military base. In general, announcement-execution intervals should be so planned as to (1) provide us time to execute the complete action and (2) be just sufficient for rational consideration by the opponent and for his preparation of reciprocation. However, the announcement of each intention should include explicit statement of the proposed date of execution (or completion); otherwise, both announcements and executions lose much of their force.

Identifying each action with our general policy of reducing and controlling world tensions also serves to clarify and direct the opponent's interpretation of our moves. But it does more than this. It serves to tie the diverse steps in many spheres and different loci together in the opponent's mind, thereby augmenting their cumulative pressure on him toward reciprocation and toward accepting the genuineness of our intent. This repeated identification of each initiative with the policy as a whole has the same communication effect as the repetition of a product name in advertising; in this case we are trying to convince the "buyer" that we are honest in our intent to reduce tensions, and that every action we take stands as evidence for this honesty.

Public announcement of our intentions is recommended as a means of enlisting the pressures of world opinion toward reciprocation. Since both the Communists and the West see themselves as competing for the good will of uncommitted nations around the world, pressures from neutrals for both sides to join in the march toward peace could become very significant—particularly as GRIT is continued. In effect, we would be saying to the Russians, "You have been talking long and loud about general and complete disarmament. You say you sincerely desire peaceful coexistence. All right. We are offering you a chance to take small, but steady and consistent, steps toward that goal along with us. The whole world is watching us—shall we move?" Furthermore, many of our actions would invite reciprocation from multiple nations or even all nations, and public announcement provides a common framework for all. And last, but not least, we would be offering the world as a whole a new model for international behavior in the nuclear age.

(h) *In their announcement, unilateral initiatives should include explicit invitation to reciprocation in some form.*

In the recent history of Russo-American relations there have been a number of unilateral gestures made by both sides, but they have been largely abortive. Why? In part this has been because they were not elements in a consistent policy and therefore were never disentangled from the cold war. But in part it was also because a total psychological framework, including explicit invitation to reciprocation, was never applied. It was further because these isolated actions were, in truth, not intended to be tension-reducing—they were taken primarily for other reasons.

In traveling about this country and some foreign countries, I have often talked about GRIT. Someone invariably says that WE have made unilateral gestures but THEY have failed to reciprocate, so how can we expect the policy to work now? An American will say, "Why, right after World War II the United States made the greatest unilateral reduction of armed forces in history—but the Russians didn't reciprocate." But what is not mentioned is the fact that there were strong internal pressures to "get our boys back home" and at the same time we were busily and exclusively producing nuclear weapons. Once a member of the Russian Embassy was in my audience. At the conclusion of the talk someone asked him what he thought about GRIT. "Why," he said, "that is just what we have been doing all the time!" I think that if the reader looks over the criteria I have been discussing in this and the preceding section, he will agree that *neither* side has actually adopted GRIT as a serious and consistent policy.

Initiation and reciprocation need not be the same in kind or even equal in quantity. *It is the fact that reciprocation in some form, tension-reducing in intent, is expected that must be made explicit.* It may be the same or different in kind, depending on the nature of our initiative. We could request that our diplomatic recognition of Communist China be reciprocated in kind; but our denuclearizing of a military base in the Pacific could not be reciprocated in kind by the Chinese—not right now, at least. Reciprocation need not be objectively balanced in quantity. We might expect our reduction of military personnel in West Berlin to be matched by an equal reduction of Russian military personnel in East Berlin; but we should not expect the closed Russian society to match our own open society in the absolute amount of inspection allowed. In other words, the burden of the same rule may be quite different in two different countries.

It is the tension-reducing impact of initiation and reciprocation that must be roughly equated. Therefore, in a sense, it is the spirit of GRIT which must be accepted and shared. However, "spirit" is a difficult thing for political strategists to cope with, and we shall want to inquire more closely into this problem of evaluating the significance of reciprocations in a later section on strategy and tactics. It should also be noted that in some cases reciprocation might be left open-ended, with selection of appropriate response entirely up to the opponent. Explicit invitation to reciprocation—whether specific or open-ended—serves several purposes. It encourages the opponent to consider actively tension-reducing alternatives. It assures him that we will correctly interpret his ensuing action, or at least be favorably disposed toward a nonaggressive interpretation. It indicates that we believe his motives to be parallel to ours, if not identical.

(i) *Unilateral initiatives that have been announced must be executed on schedule regardless of prior commitment by the opponent to reciprocate.*

This is the characteristic that distinguishes GRIT most clearly from traditional bargaining and negotiating procedures. We have already seen how biased perceptions of what is equable, self-fulfilling prophecies, and plain ordinary distrust—to say nothing of a number of bulky Sacred Cows—bedevil attempts at negotiating significant agreements under conditions of high tension. Since it is the nature of negotiated agreements and treaties that both sides must commit themselves before either can act, this means that our freedom of action is greatly restricted, as is the opponent's; both are hamstrung by the requirement of prior commitment.

GRIT breaks the chains of prior commitment, allowing both sides increased freedom of initiative, via unilateral action, but it substitutes a kind of *post-commitment*. The occurrence of reciprocation is the post-commitment. It is a kind of implicit, non-negotiated agreement that permits the process to keep going. If no reciprocation is forthcoming, or if reciprocations continue to be merely token in nature, then the process slows down, may have to come to a halt, or even reverse.

It is crucial, however, that actions which have been announced be carried out on schedule, regardless of the opponent's expressed intent to reciprocate, regardless of his propaganda moves, and regardless of tension-increasing events elsewhere. Our firm execution of a previously announced act, despite the opponent's threats and cries of "cold war propaganda," represents a direct contradiction of his expectation about what Capitalist warmongers will do and is therefore a significant learning experience for him. Every time we execute a previously announced action which the opponent has denounced as propaganda, his self-made prophecy is *not* being fulfilled. On the other hand, if for any reason we fail to do what we promised, and on the date set, then the credibility of GRIT goes down, both in the eyes of the opponent and in the eyes of the rest of the world. The way to regulate the policy is to reduce the significance of our initiatives, or even stop offering them for a while altogether—not welsh on our previous commitments.

(j) *Unilateral initiatives must be continued over a considerable period, regardless of immediate reciprocation or events of a tension-increasing nature elsewhere.*

It is essential that we do not stake everything on a single dramatic gesture, and then give up the policy if the enemy fails to cooperate or if a crisis develops during the interval. It may be important to begin with a fairly dramatic initiative, but even this should be worked into a continuing matrix of other actions. In an earlier section I emphasized the importance of having available a supply of potential actions, graduated in the degree of risk entailed and diversified over various spheres and loci of application. It is this supply of available tension-reducing initiatives, which can be announced and executed in patterns of overlapping cycles, that gives GRIT its cumulative power.

Given the tense atmosphere in which such a strategy would necessarily begin, it is almost certain that our early initiatives would be met with the scornful statement that "it is nothing but a cold war trick!" The fact that our early initiatives would also of necessity be small steps of minor military significance would further contribute to this interpretation. But the genuineness of our intent becomes more and more difficult to deny and rationalize as action follows announced action with the steady impact of a hammered nail. Not only is the opponent's self-fulfilling prophecy being repeatedly denied, but his bogey man conception of us (his enemy) is being consistently confounded; the machinations of his psycho-logic (ordinarily reinforced by our threatening gestures) must become more and more complex and ludicrous until they fall of their own weight. This, again, is a forced learning process that we should be able to induce unilaterally by applying GRIT.

Another reason for planning and applying series of graded initiatives is that we can confidently expect the pressure on the opponent to cumulate over such a sequence of actions. Like a snowball gathering weight and momentum as it rolls downhill, a series of diverse and individually minor initiatives, linked explicitly to a common policy, will gather significance and impact as action follows announced action. The pressure on the opponent to reciprocate will become more and more difficult to resist.

(k) *Unilateral initiatives must, wherever possible, take advantage of mutual self-interests, mutual self-restraints, and opportunities for cooperative enterprise.*

It sounds like a truism to say that reciprocation from an opponent is most likely to be obtained when the action in question is clearly in his own self-interest. It also seems rather obvious that resistance at home will be minimal when the initiative in question is also clearly in our own self-interest. These things are obvious, but the problem is to find actions that simultaneously satisfy the self-interest of both sides. Actually, there are a great many potential moves which have this property. There are actions which are more matters of human welfare than matters of national security—exchanges of scientific, medical, and cultural information, for example. There are reciprocations that are normal between friendly nations, but not between unfriendly nations—like diplomatic exchanges and the elimination of discriminative trade barriers. There are also some areas where we know the Soviets are eager to move positively and which are not to our disadvantage in the long run—for example, their eagerness to neutralize Germany and their need to expand their production of consumer goods. There are many such areas of common interest that can be discovered once we look for them.

The real problem is not the unavailability of actions that meet the criterion of mutual self-interest, but rather the psychological block against seeing them that way. The operation of psychologic on both sides makes it difficult for US to see anything that is good for THEM as being anything other than bad for ourselves. This is the familiar "if they are for it, we must be against it" mechanism. We have seen this operating in our attempts to negotiate the Berlin problem and even in reactions to more general disarmament proposals. Neanderthal thinkers on our side immediately distrust any offer or suggestion that comes from Khrushchev, on the ground that anything HE proposes must automatically be to our disadvantage—and, no doubt, the Russians view any offer on our part as designed to further our interests as against theirs.

The same source of resistance hampers the search for initiative/reciprocation pairs in areas where mutual self-restraints are already imposed. Once one starts looking, he finds many instances of both mutual and unilateral self-restraint which could serve as the foundations of initiatives on our part. For example, there is no formal rule about it, but both the United States and the U.S.S.R. have refrained from aiming their missiles in even the general direction of the other side while testing them. The Soviets have unilaterally refrained from high-altitude spy flights over our heartland, and now we are also refraining (on the basis of a reciprocative action by President Kennedy that did have a tension-reducing impact, incidentally). We unilaterally refrained from using atomic weapons in Korea when we had a virtual monopoly. Both sides continue to exercise self-restraint insofar as attempting assassinations on opponent elites is concerned. Careful study of bilateral and unilateral patterns of self-restraint should provide useful guidelines for designing programs of unilateral initiatives.

The opportunities for cooperative enterprises are legion, but again psycho-logic often prevents us from even conceiving them. One magnificent exception was the International Geophysical Year (IGY), in which physical scientists the world over (including the Communist bloc) cooperated in finding out more facts about the globe we all live on. The IGY example also illustrates mutual self-interest; there are problems in geophysics that require observations from many points on the earth's surface, and the scientists of a single nation could not handle them from their own soil. Another exception with high potential payoff is the proposal for joint space exploration. There are other cooperative endeavors in science and medicine that have been proposed—an International Health Year, for example, or Atoms for Peace. But the possibilities for cooperative enterprise are not limited to science. By unilateral initiative and reciprocation we might be able to engage the Soviets in cooperatively raising the standards of living in "have-not" countries, in alleviating famine in China, and in developing international universities.

Selecting initiatives which meet the criteria of mutual self-interest, mutual self-restraint, or mutual cooperation, and which therefore are most likely to be reciprocated, is particularly important in the early phases of GRIT. Again this comes down to the fact that this is a kind of international communicating and learning process. To get such a policy under way, we need to take actions which have the greatest likelihood of being correctly interpreted. And since in the early trials of learning it is important to have the probabilities of reinforcement as high as possible, we need to invite reciprocations that are most likely to be given, so that these correct responses can be rewarded. But to do these things, Homo

Sapiens must avoid the mental trap of assuming that what is good for THEM is necessarily bad for US.

(1) *Unilateral initiatives must be as unambiguous and as susceptible to verification as possible.*

Although it is true that even overt actions are liable to ambiguity and misinterpretation, nevertheless actions do speak louder than words, and this is one of the advantages that GRIT has over ordinary negotiations. However, by the same token, this means that the more our initiatives take the form of overt deeds rather than mere promises, the greater will be their perceived genuineness. Positive sanctions ("We will give financial support to the UN if you do") are really a form of negotiation, and they have the same requirement of prior commitment by both sides. Negative sanctions ("We will not be the first to use nuclear weapons, we will not engage in spy flights over your territory," etc.) have no visible execution or test until their failure; witness the fact that the unilaterally imposed test bans did relatively little to reduce tensions, but a great deal to increase tensions when they were broken. This does not mean that verbal sanctions are of no value, but rather that they lack the impact of overt deeds and are too easily taken back.

Our unilateral initiatives should also be unambiguous with respect to their tension-reducing intent. If the opponent clearly perceives his own external threat as being reduced by our initiating action, he in turn acquires increased degrees of freedom for action. Or, to put it another way, actions on our part which increase the opponent's sense of security simultaneously increase the degree of risk which he can take. This means that while our initiatives should not be advantageous to the opponent in terms of military aggression on his part, they must not be unequally disadvantageous to him militarily if he reciprocates. On the other hand, actions which are disadvantageous to ourselves, in the sense of military aggression on our part, do have impressive genuineness.

Finally, there is the matter of *verification.* The clearer the articulation and verifiability of our own unilateral actions, the less easily can the opponent misinterpret them (either deliberately or inadvertently) and therefore the greater the pressure on him to reciprocate. And, of course, the same shoe fits the other's foot: the clearer and more verifiable his reciprocations the more we are encouraged to continue the program. Therefore we should invite unambiguous and verifiable reciprocations wherever possible. The deactivation of a specific overseas base, with invited public observation, is more readily verifiable than an announced shift in the defense budget away from "soft" manned bombers and toward "hard" second-strike missiles. Inviting the opponent to eliminate certain tariff barriers on our goods is more immediately verifiable than inviting him to cease producing plutonium—without rather elaborate inspection arrangements, that is. And, on the matter of inspection, it should be noted that GRIT would make it possible to introduce reciprocal inspection in small, manageable, and therefore perhaps palatable packages. Wherever possible, we should invite both United Nations and opponent inspection of our actions on a unilateral basis, keeping in mind that what little we lose in the way of secrecy may be more than made up by a reduced need for secrecy, and we should invite the opponent to reciprocate in kind. This is an ideal form of verification.

STRATEGY AND TACTICS

It must be obvious by now that mounting such a "peace offensive" as this would require extraordinary sensitivity, determination, and restraint from leadership on all sides. GRIT would also require high-level strategic planning and monitoring, and a degree of tactical sophistication and flexibility demanded by neither war nor negotiation. To some this may seem like a flaw—too complicated for ordinary humans to handle. But can this be the case for a species that has conquered the atom and is about to conquer space? No, to the contrary, the complexity of GRIT must be viewed as a *challenge*. It is a challenge to man's ingenuity and social inventiveness. It is a challenge that he must meet if he is going to survive with his present physical technology.

But no individual can comprehend the complexity of such a policy in its entirety—certainly not a college professor sitting in his ivory tower, with or without the aid of the pipe clamped in his jaws. Nor could any single agency of government mount the "peace offensive." The new Arms Control and Disarmament Agency might well be responsible for the planning and monitoring of GRIT, along with key people in the Departments of Defense and State, but execution of this policy would involve all aspects of government, both administrative and legislative. This is because, as we have seen, GRIT would include much more than just military or disarmament steps; it would also include moves in diplomatic, economic, cultural, scientific, and other spheres, and thus involve most governmental agencies and the support of Congress. Needless to say, all of these diverse, yet integrated, activities would necessarily have their focus in the White House.

However, undaunted and with pipe firmly clamped in jaw, the college professor charges into the problem of strategy and tactics, hoping by his foolhardy gesture to enliven the interest of more competent men.

Planning Ahead

Americans have a way of reacting with great shock and surprise to world events, particularly those of an undesirable nature. The mass media, perhaps to enhance the sensational value of news, have a way of treating such events as if they had come "right out of the blue." But all events have their antecedents; they cast their shadows before them. Within any particular sphere and locus—for example, political events in Laos—it is possible to lay out in advance what the most probable alternative futures are. Then, keeping these alternatives in mind, it is possible to evaluate events today as they point toward one future rather than another, and then events tomorrow as they point even more strongly, or perhaps less strongly, toward that one of many futures. In this way we can not only anticipate more accurately what is going to happen, we can also be busily adapting our strategy for handling it. There is no need to be entirely shocked and surprised, and there is no need to be caught flatfooted.

It is largely *because* events are allowed to creep up on us unawares that we blow them into crises. Certainly there were ample forewarnings of what was likely to happen in Berlin. Had we been already under way with our interpretations and adaptive reactions, it might have been kept a "Berlin situation" rather than becoming a "Berlin crisis." Rather than becoming almost hypnotically fixated on this issue and dedicated to inflexible "matters of principle" even before we had carefully evaluated it, we might have already been moving to solve it.

Let us look inside the rat laboratory for a moment. We place our furry test tubes in a situation where a buzzer is always followed by an unavoidable, and rather unpleasant, shock to the footpads. For one group of animals there is some specific response they can make which will promptly turn off the shock as soon as it comes on; for the other group no "turn-it-off" response is provided, although the duration of shock is kept the same. What happens? The rats that can "control" the unpleasant event soon lose their fear of it; the rats that cannot are in a constant state of anxiety. In the same way, if we provide ourselves with ways of "controlling" (being prepared to handle) coming events, we will lose much of our hypnotic anxiety about them.

As it is, American Man, exposed to a flood of information that is sometimes conflicting and often sensational, tightens up all over and then loosens a bit and then tightens up all over again, as the waves of repeated crises pound through his media. During the periods of crisis, he becomes rigidly traditional in policy, adopting the familiar posture of threat and defiance. Those who are striving to inject fresh policy approaches often get the feeling that they are caught in the old childhood game of Red Light: if, while moving ahead, you get caught by a crisis, you must take three Giant Steps backward! People in the policy-planning agencies of government often complain that their best brains are kept so busy trying to handle the crises of the moment that they have no time left over to plan. This is a poor way to run a business. In every policy-planning agency, at least some of the best brains should be isolated from crises and devoted to forecasting and preparing for future developments.

It is also true that in times of crisis policy-makers are emotionally less capable of considering unconventional approaches, to say nothing of supporting research and development on them. So it happens that, in the periods of relative calm when policy-makers are ready at least to consider the feasibility of some new alternative, there is nothing available in carefully prepared and evaluated form. Regardless of the tides of world crises, we need to make a continuing investment in planning; we need to set aside some of our best brains for policy research and evaluation—just as major industries put men aside in well-equipped laboratories—and hope that they will come up with useful social inventions. We need to play peace games just as seriously as we play war games.

Establishing a Policy Framework

Graduated Reciprocation in Tension-reduction is not a collection of isolated acts, to be tried on like the bonnets in a lady's wardrobe as the occasion permits. Rather, it is an over-all policy, and as such it demands a complete analysis and reorientation of thinking about international relations. If our positions on questions like Algeria and Goa and our tactics in places like Berlin and Laos are to be anything other than opportunistic, then we must have an explicitly thought-out policy framework within which positions and tactics on specific issues like these can be consistently decided.

It would seem, therefore, that the first step would be the establishment of what might be called a *Strategy Planning Board*. This board should include some of the best brains from the Pentagon and the State Department, some of the best from the physical, behavioral, and social sciences, and some from industry; it should be organized within the Arms Control and Disarmament Agency and have broad liaison with the White House. The general purposes of this board would be (1) to organize and direct high-priority studies on the strategy of GRIT and on the tactics to be employed in executing it, (2) to evaluate the feasibility of GRIT in terms of the results of these studies, and (3) to apply the strategic and tactical criteria developed in this research to the formulation of programs of initiatives in specific areas.

The primary problem of strategy is the setting up and evaluation of criteria for selecting and ordering specific initiatives. Some of the criteria I suggested in the last section for maintaining national security while at the same time inducing reciprocation from an opponent could provide a beginning. Thus I would propose as minimum criteria for strategy in GRIT that our initiatives (a) do not reduce our capacity for unacceptable nuclear retaliation in case of attack, (b) do not cripple our capacity to meet limited aggression within various areas of application, (c) be graduated in risk potential according to reciprocations obtained, (d) be diversified over various spheres and loci, (e) be sincerely and explicitly designed to reduce tensions, and (f) be executed on schedule regardless of prior commitment by the opponent to reciprocate and regardless of crises. This is only a minimal set, and these are obviously open to critical discussion.

But behind the evaluation of these and other criteria must lie a great deal of research. One important direction of research would be into *psychological assumptions underlying GRIT*. What is the relation between national tension level and both rationality and flexibility in decision-making by leadership? What are contemporary American and Soviet perceptions and motivations with respect to each other, and how can GRIT be expected to modify these things? What are the major sources of tension in Soviet-American, Sino-American, Sino-Soviet, etc. relations? Is it possible to transfer the principles of individual behavior to the level of elite groups and nations at all, and if so, with what modifications?

Another important direction of research would be into *the context of unilateral initiatives* and how this context must influence choice. What are the comparative advantages of unilateral initiative *vs.* bilateral agreement under different levels of tension, in different spheres of action, in different loci (nations)? What can history tell us about the contexts within which unilateral initiatives have been successful? (History is generally written around the dramas of major military conflicts, but one suspects that along its byways he would discover many instances where GRIT has avoided armed conflict.) What are the real similarities and differences between the United States and the U.S.S.R. in ideology, in the interpretation of historical events, and in the decision-making structure, and how are these things likely to influence the interpretation of GRIT? What are likely to be the internal sources of support and resistance to such a tension-reducing policy—in this country, in allied countries, in enemy countries? How do internal and external pressures interact in the final formulation of policy decisions—in this country, in allied countries, in enemy countries?

Much of this research is scholarly, historical, and critical, but much of it also could be more quantitative and experimental in nature. There are now available, for example, techniques for simulating international relations in controllable laboratory settings, techniques for trying out many interpersonal and intergroup conflict and bargaining problems in game situations, and techniques for programming complex situations onto computers. Some of the research here is already available—in universities, in special research centers, and in government agencies—but it needs to be integrated, systematized, and brought to bear on the question of the feasibility of GRIT.

Particularly important for both planning and executing programs of unilateral initiatives is the setting up of *indexes of critical variables*—risk potential, security potential, reciprocation potential, verifiability, tension level, and psychological impact, for example. In establishing such indexes we must first agree on what the variables really are; what, for example, does "tension level" mean when applied to a nation rather than an individual? Then we must decide on the best indicators or measures of these things; how might one estimate the probable risk to our security in actions X, Y, and Z in some standard way? And, ideally, these indexes should be objective rather than subjective, even quantitative where possible.

If sequences of initiatives are to be designed for different spheres and loci, we need to be able to grade the *risk potentials* of actions both within and between different areas of action. Should the action not be reciprocated, does denuclearizing West Germany involve greater or lesser risk to our security than deactivating a "soft" base in Turkey? How much security is being risked when we make public our scientific information on man-in-space, compared, say, with eliminating trade barriers with Red China? In developing an index of risk potential we must be careful not to fall into the trap of possibilistic decision-making—that is, grading initiatives in terms of what *could* happen rather than in terms of what most probably would happen.

In order to evaluate the significance of an opponent's reciprocations, we need to develop some way of indexing the *security potential* for us in his moves. While our own initiatives may mean some security risk, reciprocations by an opponent should mean some security gain, and therefore the index here would probably be the inverse of the one above and involve the same general considerations. How much do we gain by way of national security if the Russians join us in providing technicians for the Congo? If they cut their armed forces in East Germany in half? If they reduce travel restrictions on our tourists? In making these estimations objectively we must avoid the trap of psycho-logic—depreciating the significance of their moves just because they are THEY.

In this connection, training in "role-playing" could be most useful to our own strategists.

To plan our own initiatives in such a way as to maximize the likelihood of opponent response we need to develop some index of *reciprocation potential*. What kinds of actions on our part are most likely to be reciprocated in kind? What types of invited reciprocations, whether the same in kind or quantity or not, are most likely to be accepted? To make such predictions with any degree of accuracy would demand a great deal of understanding of the present needs and motives of our opponents, as well as insightful historical studies of their past behaviors. And here, certainly, we would learn much in the process of applying GRIT —through deliberate trial and error in the early phases.

Related to the reciprocation potential of our initiatives, but also concerned with our evaluation of their reciprocating moves, is the index of *verifiability*. Some acts, as we have seen, have absolute zero verifiability—for example, a negative sanction that we will not do something unless they do it first. Other acts have immediate and uncontestable verifiability—reduction of trade barriers, shipments of food supplies, and moving the seating of Red China in the United Nations, for example. Most acts will range somewhere between these extremes. Some require inspection by an opponent (or a neutral United Nations) team, such as deactivation of bases or disengagement in Central Europe; others can only be verified indirectly, as when we say we are shifting our arms balance; and yet others are necessarily ambiguous—did we really release *all* we know scientifically about man-in-space and did the Russians *really* tell all in reciprocating? Having some index of verifiability encourages us to maximize this variable in designing our own initiatives; at the same time, it provides us with a means of gauging the significance of enemy reciprocations.

Unlike the indexes we have been considering so far, which have been concerned with initiating and reciprocating actions themselves, an index of *tension level* would try to gauge the success or failure of GRIT. The strategy as a whole is designed to reduce tensions, both at home and abroad. What is the tension level in Nation X at present? How is this level affected by our announcement of a certain initiative? Is tension level in Nation X reduced more by our announcement, our execution, or by its own reciprocation? (I would predict some tension increase upon our announcement, particularly early in the game, some tension decrease with our execution, and the most tension decrease accompanying their own reciprocation.) What about tension levels in our own country, as the initiator of the policy? Will our tensions increase as action follows announced action without obvious reciprocation? Undoubtedly. Will tensions decrease abruptly when verifiable reciprocation from the opponent does occur? Undoubtedly.

But guesswork is not enough; we need to devise sensitive indexes of tension levels in nations. There are many possibilities here. National tension increase is typically accompanied by pressures toward solidarity ("close ranks"), by inflexibility in public posture ("we must stand firm"), by fixation on certain issues ("Berlin is the key"), by emotional stereotyping ("Capitalist warmongers," "Communist slavery"), and by all the dynamics of psycho-logic ("we are all things noble; they are all things evil"). Content analyses of the mass media in various countries should provide indexes here, along with analyses of statements by public figures. But there are other measures, too—for example, shifts in tourism, spending for luxury goods, long-term savings, buying of reading materials about the other country, and positions taken at the United Nations. And then, of course, there are the more usual diplomatic thermometers. By looking back over recent history, spotting periods of relatively high and low tension in various nations, and then testing these possible measures for their sensitivity, we certainly could come up with useful indexes of tension level.

Finally, we have the matter of *psychological impact*. The psychological impact of an action does not necessarily depend upon its military significance, although it may. Certain announcements and subsequent actions have the property of being dramatic, of catching the eyes and hearts of people all over the world; others do not. Where the reduction of trade barriers may be psychologically pretty drab, the announcement that we would move the seating of Red China would be quite dramatic. The cycling of the first Sputnik through our skies had a tremendous psychological impact, much more than the militarily more significant shift toward conventional warfare on our part. The announcement that, as of January 1, we would make the DEW-line warning system bidirectional—warning the Soviets of attacks from us as well as warning us of attacks from them—also would have elements of drama. Similarly, the announcement of an International Health Year, on the model of IGY, should have more impact on world attention than an equivalent increase in our foreign aid. The Peace Corps had the same dramatic appeal. It should be possible to pretest the probable psychological impact of various initiatives by getting reactions from small samples of people in countries around the world; we could even use foreign students studying in this country to help here.

Guided by general policy criteria, supported by extensive background research, and aided by objective indexes of the most critical variables, we would now be ready to get GRIT onto a set of blueprints for action. This would mean preparing what might be called a *Sphere/Locus Form Chart*. Each row in this chart would specify a different locus of application—the Soviet Union, Communist China, Southeast Asia, Central Europe, Latin America, Africa, and so forth, as well as Nations in General. Each column would specify a different sphere of action—Arms Management (including disengagement), Disarmament, Inspection and Controls, Diplomacy, Law, Economics, Science (including Medicine), Culture (including Education and Communication), and so forth. Each of the "cells" of this chart would specify a particular area (sphere and locus of action) within which to devise initiatives and invited reciprocations. For example: Arms Management with respect to Southeast Asia, Cultural actions vis-à-vis Latin America, Scientific initiatives relating to Communist China, Disarmament vis-à-vis the Soviet Union, Economic actions affecting Central Europe, and so forth. Some of the cells would be of trivial significance and hence be left empty, such as Disarmament with respect to Latin America.

The problem at this point would be to rate each proposed action in each cell against the indexes described above—its risk potential, its reciprocation potential, its verifiability, and its psychological significance—as well as each proposed reciprocation in terms of its security potential for us and its verifiability. Then the initiatives in each cell would be ordered according to their indexes and the available contextual information. The general rule for ordering would be that earlier actions should minimize risk while maximizing reciprocation potential, verifiability, and psychological impact.

Such a "form chart" for initiatives in various spheres and at various loci would be only a skeleton program, constantly under revision as a function of changing opponent moves and other circumstances. However, it is the availability of graded actions across such a broad front and involving so many spheres of action that would give our tacticians the flexibility they would need to keep such a policy moving.

No matter how jaunty the angle of his pipe, this college professor, as I said before, does not have anything like the information (much of it classified) required to detail a complete sphere/locus chart for GRIT. The accompanying figure merely suggests some of the initiatives that might appear in only two of the cells. ARMS MANAGEMENT/SOVIET UNION: (1) Displacement of nuclear production and missile sites away from civilian population centers; reciprocation in kind invited; progressive inspection of population areas invited as cleared. (2) DEW-line (distant early warning system) made bidirectional and Soviets invited to

SPHERE ⟶ LOCUS ↓	ARMS MANAGEMENT	CULTURAL INITIATIVES
SOVIET UNION	(1) Nuclear displacement (2) Bidirectional DEW-line (3) Military base for international university in Pakistan (4) Polaris beyond target range (5) Disengagement in West Germany	
LATIN AMERICA		(1) Talent tours (2) Scientist and scholar exchange (3) Support and privilege for Latin tourists (4) Uncensored Sunday page by Latin journalists (5) Exchange of public opinion researchers

share information; reciprocation open-ended. (3) Military base in Pakistan deactivated with inspection and an international university activated on same site; participation of all nations in support and staffing invited, under United Nations auspices; pullback of Soviet ground forces in area requested as reciprocation. (4) Polaris submarines to be kept mobile, but beyond targeting range; reciprocation in kind requested (with observers in communication centers). (5) West Germany denuclearized and NATO forces there cut in half; equivalent reciprocation requested. CULTURAL INITIATIVES/LATIN AMERICA: Reciprocation in kind requested for (1) talent tours of Latins in this country, (2) invitations of Latin-American scientists and scholars to teach in this country, (3) special tourist privileges, (4) Sunday page in major newspapers prepared without censorship by South American journalists, and (5) export of public opinion experts and equipment for surveys.

Playing It by Ear

Another essential difference between GRIT and negotiated agreements must now be pointed out. In agreements on disarmament or disengagement arrived at by negotiation, all of the steps must be laid out in advance; the phases and stages are specified in the agreement, and the parties then proceed to move in unison down the defined path—provided the negotiations are successful and provided that nothing happens during the procession to send them scurrying up the arms race spiral again. Graduated Reciprocation in Tension-reduction is another kind of process altogether. It is more like courtship than marriage, more like a conversation than a prayer. Rather than marching in unison, the players of GRIT move in complicated steps of their own, each keeping his eyes on the moves of the other, and leading or following, now one, now the other, as the case may be. But the goal of the improvised dance is the same as the goal of the stately procession: a more secure and peaceful world.

As a matter of fact, the tactics of GRIT would be very similar to those of improvisation in good jazz music. To improvise effectively and creatively in jazz, the soloist must know the actual melody (even though he never plays it as written), he must know the progression of basic chords, he must keep an ear on what the others in the group are doing simultaneously (particularly the rhythm section), and he must remember what the other solo-ists have done in earlier choruses, so that he can carry on and perhaps intensify the atmosphere they have been creating. Know-ing all these things simultaneously—or perhaps better, feeling all these things intuitively—our soloist then selects the particular notes for his own contribution. He selects notes not singly but in thematic sequences, not rigidly according to an entirely pre-conceived plan but flexibly in terms of what he himself has said before and what the others are now saying to him. Sometimes he makes beautiful music.

Now observe the problems of the GRIT tactician. He knows the general strategy of GRIT, its guiding principles and its aims; he is by now familiar with the rules by which one selects actions designed to induce reciprocation while still maintaining ade-quate security; our tactician has been keeping an eye on what has been happening in various spheres and loci, allies as well as neutrals, and thus he knows the context within which his own moves must be made; particularly, he has been observing and evaluating what the opponent has been doing in response to his previous actions. Knowing all these things, the GRIT tactician selects new initiatives of his own—not in isolation and not ac-cording to some prearranged plan, but in new sequences, flexi-bly designed to intensify the atmosphere of mutual trust and understanding.

It would be the sensitive and difficult job of a *Tactics Staff* to design programs of unilateral initiatives for execution in each succeeding phase of the policy. These programs or sequences of initiatives would be selected from those available in the Sphere/Locus Form Chart (which would have to be under continuous revision), and each program would consist of actions drawn from diverse "cells" in the chart. The particular selections and order-ings would depend upon the context of the moment, the stage of the process, and the previous reciprocative behavior of the op-ponent. One of the futures for man described in the first chapter traced one hypothetical program of initiatives. This tactical staff would be aided in its complex operation by a large supporting organization; using high-speed computers, extensive "intelli-gence" from all over the world, including data for tension-level indexes in most countries, would be synthesized and interpreted for them. Intensive communication with the opponent, both private and public, would have to be maintained in both directions—intelligence as to effects and messages as to intents. This would serve both to reduce the likelihood of disruption due to misinterpretation and to facilitate effective action and reaction.

What rules, what criteria, would guide the tactics of GRIT? The characteristics I gave in the preceding section could provide a beginning here. Our unilateral initiatives should (g) be graduated in risk potential according to reciprocations obtained, (h) be unpredictable by the opponent as to sphere, locus, and time of execution prior to our announcement (it is here, not in the general nature of our policy, that secrecy must be maintained), (i) be announced publicly prior to execution and identified as part of the general policy, (j) include explicit invitation to reciprocation in some form, (k) be continued in sequences over a considerable period regardless of reciprocation or crises, and (l) be as unambiguous and susceptible to verification as possible. Some of these criteria would also be subject to critical evaluation. Is prior announcement tactically superior to simultaneous announcement and execution (and for all actions)? Is explicit invitation to reciprocation superior to open-ended requests?

There are other tactical problems that would demand preliminary research and evaluation. There is the question of *timing* our actions: is it better to announce a series of moves simultaneously or to have them delivered in a planned sequence? There is the matter of *cycling and overlap:* some actions require considerable time for the complete cycle between announcement and completion of reciprocation, others very little, and this means overlap among initiatives and reciprocations; is this advantageous or disadvantageous, and under what conditions? For example, could we find ourselves in the position of wanting to slow down when we still had several significant actions to fulfill? And what about *covert negotiations?* Would it be a good idea to "sound out" our allies and the neutrals, as well as our opponents, informally and privately before entering on such a policy—or perhaps before announcing particular acts? While this might help us select the most effective moves, it also might serve to damp our initiative. Then there is the question of the *involvement of the United Nations:* what types of action would be best mediated through this international body? Yet another is the problem of *roles:* who announces our initiatives—the President? Always? What is the role of the press?

There are two tactical devices that deserve special attention. One is the possibility of *displacing initiative onto nonpolar powers.* When our own motives might be highly suspect (particularly in the early stages), it might be most effective to have the initiative come unilaterally from a nonpolar nation (for example, Canada, India, Yugoslavia) than from either the United States or the U.S.S.R. Then we could promptly reciprocate, thereby putting pressure on our opponents to reciprocate as well. This tactic has other, less obvious advantages: since initiative would seem to come from elsewhere, it would serve to "appease the nonappeasers"; being displaced, it would inhibit the "cold war trick" response; coming from a nonpolar power, it would side-step the rationalizations of psycho-logic; and, since we would be prepared to reciprocate anyway, it would guarantee cooperative action from at least two nations as a model.

The other tactic I want to suggest is *the use of "atmosphere probes."* By this I mean the occasional use of low-risk but high-verifiability initiatives to sound out the opponent's readiness to cooperate. These "probes" would be more in the way of estimates of tension level than actions designed to alter tension level significantly. Examples would be inviting Soviet participation in an East-West conference on psychological factors in international conflict, offering to trade 100 tractors with Cuba for 100 tons of tobacco (or whatever a fair trade might be), inviting the Soviets to expand the number of their consulates in American cities and requesting them to reciprocate, offering to sink publicly a couple of old battleships and asking them to do the same, and so forth.

There are many types of research that can be applied to tactical problems. One is *historical:* we would want to look closely into the past history of national conflicts to determine what tactics seem to have worked in the past. Another type of research would be *naturalistic:* it is possible to observe the effectiveness of various tactics in other group conflict situations, such as gang warfare, business competition, labor-management strife, and even limited international conflicts (using Cuba as an experimental station, for example). Perhaps most valuable would be the *sim-*

ulation of international conflicts within laboratory situations where the variables we are interested in can be most tightly controlled and manipulated: if GRIT were being "played" by a group of "nations" (college students), what would be the difference between prior *vs.* simultaneous announcement of initiatives by one side? What would be the difference between displaced *vs.* direct initiation in a bipolar power situation? The same simulated "gaming" of GRIT could be used as an effective training ground and selection device for our own tacticians. Under these mock-up conditions they could learn what works and what does not; we could see which tacticians develop the necessary sensitivity and flexibility. And we could even use the simulation situation to pretest our possible initiatives at each stage in actual execution of the policy—that is, by duplicating in the game situation the actual sequence of events up to the present point in time, and then observing the impacts of different tactics upon the "enemy."

Finally, the tactics of GRIT would require that we carefully assess the reciprocative behavior of our opponents, in order to determine how fast or how slow to continue the process. Since the task would be similar to that of the original Strategy Planning Board, essentially the same personnel might be involved. But the problem here is to evaluate opponent reciprocations. There are two rather different questions involved here: one concerns the genuineness of the opponent's reciprocations, which seems to come down to the adequacy of intelligence in the usual military sense; the other concerns the significance of his reciprocations, and this seems to be a matter for strategic analysis, in the usual military sense.

To enhance genuineness, both the initiator's unilateral acts and the reciprocations requested of the opponent should be as unambiguous and as susceptible to verification as possible. One way of encouraging this is to include provisions for adequate and specific inspection in both our own initiatives and our requested reciprocations. There is a hidden psychological persuader here: if the opponent accepts our unilateral invitation for him to inspect some specific action by appropriately limited means, then it becomes difficult for him to deny us the same privilege subsequently. Bearing in mind that this can also be a source of resistance to reciprocation on his part, however, we should try to select early initiatives that would involve minimum inspection, particularly of the kind that might be interpretable as espionage.

But, as we have seen, there are many types of initiatives that are necessarily somewhat ambiguous, and the same applies to reciprocations. The problem here is to maximize the communication aspect of "intelligence" and minimize the espionage aspect. We can set precedents and provide models. When we have announced and executed a somewhat ambiguous or hard-to-verify action, we can encourage full media coverage and public discussion (for example, of a budgetary shift from "soft" to "hard" retaliatory capacity) and we can offer supporting bona fide actions (for example, emphasizing the large number of military transport flights between West Germany and the United States after our announcement of reductions in armed forces in Europe). Another subtle psychological factor operates here as well: if the opponent is *not* reciprocating honestly and his actions are *not* bona fide, then we can confidently expect that his (projected) suspicion and distrust of us, and hence his tension level, will not go down; this fact should be evident in our indexes of his tension level and in his responses to our "atmosphere probes."

As to the *significance* of reciprocations, two criteria should be kept in mind. First, over the long run, but not necessarily at every moment, the risk potential in our initiatives should be roughly compensated for by the increased security gained through the opponent's reciprocations. Second, tension-decreasing steps in one area must be balanced against the total level of tension-increasing and tension-decreasing events in all areas. The problem of the strategist here is complex—the aid of computers in synthesizing information from many areas would undoubtedly be required—but this sort of strategic analysis is going on all the time anyhow.

There are several points on which our strategists should be forewarned. For one thing—national pride being what it is—we could confidently expect that much of the reciprocation by the other side would actually appear as their initiative inviting our reciprocation. As long as their actions are in the direction we want, this makes little difference; however, it does mean that our strategists must be flexible and quick-witted in estimating the significance of such steps and in preparing our reciprocations (further initiatives). In other words, just as with the arms race, once such a reciprocative international process is under way, it becomes impossible to determine who is acting and who is re-acting, and it makes no difference. For another thing—psycho-logic being what it is—our strategists will be prone to underestimate the significance of opponent reciprocations and overestimate the sig-nificance of our initiatives. Therefore, within reasonable limits of security and particularly in the early phases, we should lean over backward in our evaluations. And last, it should be kept in mind that even token initiatives and reciprocations of minimal real sig-nificance would be of considerable psychological value in getting GRIT under way.

There is another responsibility our strategists would have. This is the preparation of *fall-back positions*. For each initiative we consider making, we should ask ourselves in what possible ways it might be taken advantage of by the opponent, and we should be prepared in advance to respond appropriately. For example, at the time we announce our intention to withdraw military forces from Quemoy and Matsu and turn them over to Communist China (after all, these islands are as close to mainland China as Martha's Vineyard and Nantucket are to mainland Massachusetts), we should be moving naval forces toward that area in preparation to resist encroachment should it occur before the date announced for completion of evacuation. As a matter of fact, for each proposed initiative on our part, a strategy board would have to anticipate several alternative reactions from the opponent and be prepared with our subsequent response: they try to encroach—we are pre-pared to resist; they make no reciprocation or only token recipro-cation—we are prepared to continue with small-risk steps; they make a significant and bona fide reciprocation—we are prepared with a more significant next step of our own. In this way we monitor GRIT in terms of our own evaluations of the reciproca-tive behavior of the other.

Forging the World of Tomorrow

One of the main sources of resistance to disarmament in this country is the fear held by many Americans that the Com-munist way of life would easily win out in a disarmed world. "Look at the map," these people say. "Look at the way the Red areas have been spreading *without* war. Imagine what would happen if we were to lay down our arms. Imagine how quickly

Communism would sweep over the world if we weren't contain-
ing them with our atomic weapons." The truth of the matter is
probably almost the opposite of this. Our dominance in nuclear
weaponry may have inhibited the spread of Communism by
military means, but it certainly has not helped us much in the
everyday battles for men's minds on the economic and political
fronts. As a matter of fact, our concentration on military aid to
underdeveloped and uncommitted countries, at the expense of
penetrating economic, social, and cultural aid, has often created
and maintained empty shells of freedom—forms without substance—just waiting to be pricked. We have not been fighting the
real war.

But now look more closely at this real war for a moment.
Strangely enough, it is not a war that we want to "win" in the
usual sense. Rather, we want to prolong this conflict while men
live and learn, confident that in the long run they will freely
choose our way and not the Communist way. We do not want to
impose our way of life on people who are not ready for it. Rather,
we want them to work themselves into it the hard way, because
this is the only way they will understand and cherish it. But this
means that we must not allow them to become frozen too early
into any pattern—certainly not the Communist pattern—which
would severely restrict their freedom to improvise and experiment. If people are to learn, they must be free to change, to make
trials, and to experience both failures and successes. This means
freedom from external domination, political, economic, or cultural.

In the real war with Communism, means are just as important as are ends. Some of the expressed goals of Communism
are consistent with our own. Take this principle, for example:
"From each according to his ability; to each according to his
need"; how different, except for stress, is this from our own belief
in unselfish public service by those who have the ability to serve
or from our own support of public welfare legislation (milk and
hot lunches for schoolchildren, social security benefits, medical
care for the aged)? But we must insist that the *means* by which
social change is brought about be acceptable, by education rather
than brainwashing, by trade rather than infiltration, by votes
rather than subversion, by law rather than force. This distinction

between ends and means is the bulwark of our own liberties; any end is debatable, it says in effect, but the means of securing it must be constitutional.

How can GRIT help us forge the world of tomorrow? It comes down to the substance of our unilateral initiatives and requested reciprocations. We should select actions whose long-run impact will be to increase the freedoms of individuals in relation to their governments. We should select actions that will provide models for how change is to be brought about. By making our own actions conform to standards of decency in international relations, we may be able to induce similar behavior from others. By submitting ourselves to a code of international ethics, we may set precedents that others will find difficult to evade. If we want a disarmed world in which our way of life can not only survive but thrive, then we must literally create its conditions in the process of achieving it. THEREFORE:

(m) *Our initiatives and requested reciprocations should, wherever feasible, involve transfer of sovereignty from national to international auspices.*

I have already expressed my belief that technological developments in communications, transportation, weaponry, and all other forms of group interaction have made some form of world government not only feasible but absolutely essential for survival in the nuclear age. Riding the crest of nationalism, leaders both here and elsewhere in the world have not attended to this "writing on the wall"; failing to perceive or comprehend this message, they keep striving to attain both international security and national autonomy simultaneously. These are incompatible goals in a nuclear age. Transfer of military capabilities to some international peace-keeping machinery is, as we have seen, an essential element in all disarmament plans, Soviet as well as American. It is crucial that our unilateral initiatives and requested reciprocation also serve, step by step, to strengthen international organizations.

The United Nations is the major, although not the only, international political organization in today's troubled world. Born on the stony bed of nationalism, weaned on the violent transition from colonialism to independence of underdeveloped areas, caught in the middle of the cold war between its Eastern and

Western parents, and not even fully formed by virtue of the exclusion of Germany and Communist China, the United Nations has had a bitter childhood. It has been used more as a propaganda platform and debating society than as an international government. Nevertheless, even this function has been valuable. Beyond this it has acted to preserve the peace in a number of potentially explosive conflict situations and, through various agencies like UNICEF and UNESCO, it has been striving persistently to create conditions of international understanding and well-being.

Today the United Nations is struggling through the crises of its adolescence. Unable to satisfy the nationalistic self-interests of all members—both by design and in justice—this international organization is now being threatened by withdrawal of financial support, by demands for radical reorganization, and even by possible dismemberment. Major schemes for international order and security seem to be born in the aftermaths of great wars—the League of Nations after World War I and the United Nations after World War II—and if the United Nations disintegrates through lack of world support, we can be sure that no substitute will be found before another, incomparably more devastating, war has swept across our planet.

The developmental pangs of world government today are closely analogous to those suffered by our own government when thirteen more or less autonomous colonies were trying to become the United States. The world situation today can be viewed in terms of the shifting interest and voting blocs that characterized our own early history: the industrial Northeast *vs.* the agricultural West and South on some issues, the "free" North *vs.* the "slave" South on others, and so on. As the federal government has grown stronger, we have come to decide issues more in terms of national than regional self-interest, have come to expect to lose on some issues while winning on others, and, perhaps most important, have become organized into competing groups that transcend rather than adhere to geographical state lines: liberal *vs.* conservative, labor *vs.* management, consumer *vs.* producer, and farmer *vs.* manufacturer. One can envision the time when farmers in Russia, China, India, Australia, and the United States would find more in common (and exert influence upon their United Nations representatives in common) than among their own countrymen. Indeed, the conflict today between the ex-colonial powers and the underdeveloped areas (including the United States vis-à-vis Latin America and the U.S.S.R. vis-à-vis China and her satellites) is similar to that between the wealthy and industrialized Northeast and the poorer and more agricultural South and West of our own nineteenth century.

The crucial difference between then and now lies in the existence of a strong central government. How can we behave so as to strengthen the United Nations, the World Court, and other international organizations? One way is to submit ourselves to the rulings of such bodies. A first unilateral step in this direction would be to repeal the Connolly Amendment, which, in effect, says that this government will not be bound by such rulings. Some will argue that we cannot do this—because we might lose some cases. Our United States would not have long endured had every self-interest group so behaved. As Roger Fisher has pointed out,[2] when Congress gave the Court of Claims power to enter judgments against the United States, there were strong objections to the nation subjecting itself to a system where it might lose cases. But more people realized that the nation would gain in the long run by having its disputes settled fairly. How would we gain by submitting our disputes to international legal bodies, *particularly* disputes where we sometimes lose? By firmly establishing the precedent of a powerful nation subjecting itself to the rule of international law, and thereby making it more difficult for other nations to evade the same legal procedure. "It may be appeasement to give in to a neighbor's demand. It is never appeasement to give in to a judge."

Another way in which our initiatives can gradually strengthen the United Nations is by unilaterally submitting developments of the future to its authority. This applies particularly to developments in the exploration and use of outer space, because outer space, certainly, belongs to the planet as a whole. Thus we could unilaterally invite United Nations authorization and inspection of space shots of a scientific, as opposed to a military, nature; we could sponsor a United Nations authority over the use of commu-

---

[2] Roger Fisher, "Do We Want to 'Win' the Cold War?" *Bulletin of the Atomic Scientists*, 1962, *18*, 33-35.

nications satellites and invite reciprocation—this is certain to be a source of irritation and conflict in the future without such international control. Furthermore, in our programs of initiatives and reciprocations, we could include steps designed to shift research and development in the basic sciences from national to international auspices under the model of IGY, particularly research having military implications. Beyond strengthening the United Nations, initiatives of this sort would have the added advantage of giving full rein to the creativeness of our scientists while at the same time gradually reducing the unstabilizing impacts of their breakthroughs upon international relations.

(n) *Our initiatives and requested reciprocations should, wherever feasible, be designed to reduce the imbalance between "have" and "have-not" countries.*

The major revolution of our time is the surge of previously colonial and primarily supportive areas and peoples toward social, political, and economic independence. This is at once a continuation of the industrial revolution, carried on the wings of communication and transportation technology, and a continuation of our own sociopolitical revolution in the relation between individual and state. The resulting conflict—finding expression yesterday in the emancipation of India from British rule, today in Cuba, the Congo, and Indonesia, and tomorrow perhaps in South Africa and Latin America—is actually at right angles to the cold war between Communism and the Free World. No matter how much WE and THEY try to force the struggles of the "have-not" countries into the mold of our psycho-logic, they refuse to play this game; rather, they understandably try to play one polar power against the other in furthering their own aims. It is also obvious that supporting this revolution puts the Soviets in less of a dilemma than ourselves, yet support it we must, despite our ties to the former colonial powers.

How can United States initiative smooth the transition from "have-not" to "have"? The answer comes down to how we handle the question of foreign aid: how much we invest in it, how successful we are in disentangling economic aid from internal profiteering, from political manipulation, and from military suffocation, how well we are able to create involvement and commitment on the part of local populations. In the past, much of our foreign aid has been used to support the local status quo and, through diversion and even downright graft, has often served to increase the gulf between "have" and "have-not" people *within* the countries receiving our aid. Unfortunately, aid has often been directed more by commercial interests at home than by economic needs abroad—and we may find thousands of tractors rusting and useless because technical training did not accompany them, because they were obviously ill-suited to rice paddies, or because the populace was not attitudinally prepared for them. Also unfortunately, we find much aid in the form of military supplies the local people do not really want to use in a war they neither comprehend nor care about.

Could the United States afford to underwrite the economic development of the rest of the world? In a recent book, Seymour Melman claims it could.[3] I am not an economist myself and therefore cannot evaluate his position, but I can give you the essence of his argument:

The achievement of rapid industrialization with freedom is frustrated by the need to accumulate industrial resources out of the meager means of impoverished peasants. For this method, the ruthless police measures of the Soviet and especially the Chinese economies are well-suited, indeed essential. But the United States can underwrite the capital cost of industrialization. It can make industrial capital into a virtually "free good." The United States is the only industrial center in the world that has large unused production and labor resources. . . . The cost of the peace race will amount, at maximum, to about 10 per cent of America's gross national product. A production increase of this size is attainable now, even while carrying the arms burden. . . . *Already strained, the Soviet economy is incapable of the same feat as that of the United States. . . . [Therefore] the Soviets will be compelled to seek disarmament in order to compete in a peace race. . . . The peace race can be started by the United States solely on its own decision* [pp. 65-66].

Even if one might argue about our capacity to underwrite economic development while still maintaining an arms race, there seems to be no doubt we could do it if military expenditures were reduced (thereby, of course, easing the transition from a war to a peace economy). Melman supports this argument with

---

[3] Seymour Melman, *The Peace Race*, Ballantine, 1961.

a number of impressive comparisons between military and peace-time expenditures: four attack submarines at 180,000,000 dollars equals United States foreign donations of agricultural commodities through all voluntary agencies in fiscal 1959; one Polaris submarine plus its missiles at 122,600,000 dollars roughly equals total United States technical cooperation within Point Four in 1961; the Atomic Energy Commission appropriations (mostly military) of 2,686,560,000 dollars for 1961 is even larger than the total government investment in TVA over a period of 24 years, 1933-57. The question is not so much *could* the American people underwrite the economic development of the world if relieved of the tensions of the arms race, but *would* they—and this seems to be more a psychological question.

Beyond a trivial quibble over terminology (I much prefer the image of a deliberate march toward peace to that of a frantic race toward it) there are several weaknesses in Melman's proposal. For one thing, people have a way of resenting help that is forced on them. Melman recognizes this problem of motivating people to make effective use of opportunities for industrialization, but says little about how to solve it. Resistances to forced industrialization may go deep into the political, religious, and social roots of a culture; witness the problems of introducing modern methods in India. There is also the prevalent image of "Uncle Santa Claus"; rather than perceiving economic aid as a means to self-improvement through indigenous effort, many people see it simply as "gifts" of a more or less obligatory sort. For another thing, there is something of the use of a whip in Melman's proposal. Economic aid is to be used as a weapon in the cold war, both to force underdeveloped countries to adopt our way of life and to force the Soviet Union to seek disarmament in order to compete. One can see where the underdeveloped countries might take a dim view of aid proffered with such strings attached and where the Soviet Union might respond with aggression rather than disarmament under such pressure.

This is where GRIT seems to come in. Melman's proposals are all initiative and no reciprocation. In order to develop self-motivated industrial development in "have-not" countries it will be necessary to work through reciprocative endeavors, even though they may be imbalanced at first, that lead toward mutual interdependencies rather than toward one-way dependencies upon the United States. This is just as necessary for morale as it is for ultimate stability. Devising reciprocative economic enterprises may require considerable ingenuity, but the end result should be well worth the effort. Similarly, with respect to the Soviet Union (relatively speaking, a "have" country), the more our unilateral initiatives toward economic development of "have-not" countries can enlist their reciprocative participation, the more stable will be such development and the less danger there will be of increasing, rather than decreasing, world tensions. After all, neither the United States nor the U.S.S.R. will be of much use to the rest of the world if their industrial might is extinguished in a nuclear war. And finally, the very gradualness of GRIT should serve to ease the transitions—on our part, from an arms-race economy to a peacetime economy, and on the part of others, from feudal or tribal organizations to fully industrialized states.

(o) *Our initiatives and requested reciprocations should, wherever feasible, be designed to strengthen democratic as against totalitarian ways of life.*

As we have seen, economic aid to "have-not" countries—the underwriting of their industrial development—cannot take place in a vacuum. It will be accepted and will be effective only to the extent that other conditions are changed in course. Furthermore, industrialization can follow the Communist model rather than our own, and many countries seem to see in this model a more rapid, if perhaps more politically dangerous, means to their ends. How can we use GRIT to encourage choices in the direction of our model, and thereby help create a world of tomorrow in which disarmament can be compatible with the security of our way of life?

Economic sufficiency. This, as Melman shows, is one way. When people exist near a bare subsistence level, little energy is left over for the development of those uniquenesses—in experience, in dwelling, in travel, in dress, and the like—which make people important to themselves as individual human beings. But this is not the only way. What are some of the other fundamental supports of a way of life in which the individual human being has freedom and dignity, and the state exists to further these ends?

Social and legal equality. Totalitarian systems display gross inequalities in civil, political, and social rights—based on the distribution of power, if nothing else. Economic power, as we see even in our own country, can also contribute to social inequality. There is much that we can do unilaterally in our own country to reinforce this ideal; it is hard to convince people of colored (nonwhite) races—the vast majority of peoples on the globe—that we really mean what we say about social equality when we obviously do not practice it at home. The behavior of our own nationals in other countries, whether members of diplomatic staffs, the Peace Corps, or just everyday tourists, can also contribute to the same end. Our initiatives and requested reciprocations, where relevant, should be designed with these things in mind.

Educational opportunity. Limited or biased education prevents people from acquiring the tools they need to better their own conditions. It is not enough to open the doors of our own universities to students from other countries; we must also help establish universities in their own cities. Unilaterally we can invite scholars and students from Ghana and India to our educational institutions, but we should also request that they reciprocate by inviting our scholars and students to work with them in their own lands. Building the interdependencies which create a stabilized world is a two-way street. On the same theme, our initiatives in providing educators, technicians, and experts (in government and law, in agriculture, in industry, in science) should be accompanied by invitations to the other "have" countries like Russia and France to participate, preferably through United Nations auspices.

Information flow. The free flow of information, both within and across national boundaries and both among individuals and via the mass media, provides the diversity of opinion in which lies the vitality of democratic institutions—the freedom of choice people need to govern themselves. We could, for example, unilaterally invite correspondents from other nations, allied, neutral, and enemy, to prepare materials on crucial world situations from their own point of view, to be published in our media without censorship (although with clear indication as to source); but we should also request reciprocation from their mass media. Such exchanges might start as brash propaganda attempts, but this would almost certainly, because of its ineffectiveness, develop into more accurate information exchange. One of the most important bases for stability between groups is mutual communication and understanding; this would also serve to develop common interests and viewpoints that cut across national boundaries.

These are only a few of the areas within which our initiatives and requested reciprocations could serve our long-term interests and help to forge the kind of world in which we would want to live. Of course, the main thing that isolates communities and prevents understanding is *external threat*. It is perceived threat from outside the group that impels people to accept subservience to the state and to forgo individual freedoms, in the interest of what they see as the common goal—security. In today's bipolar power situation, mutual threat perceptions have led both sides to erect "iron curtains" through which only carefully metered driblets of information can pass. Under such conditions, the variable most under our control is perceived external threat, and therefore this must be the focus of our strategy. We can behave so as to raise this threat or so as to lower it, and we can do it abruptly or in gradual stages. It is here, of course, that GRIT applies most directly.

However, the other conditions that support totalitarian ways of life we have been discussing can also be influenced by the substance of the acts we select and by the strategy and tactics of applying them. Tension-reducing moves can soften the "iron curtain" and permit more direct influence to be applied. We must also keep in mind the fact that liberalizing forces of considerable magnitude have been developing in Russia and in countries within her sphere of influence, particularly since the death of Stalin and his final dethronement from the circle of Soviet Saints. If the cold war mentality is the primary factor that is inhibiting these spontaneous liberalizing forces, then anything that serves to reduce world tensions should release these pent-up internal pressures and contribute to the kind of disarmed world we want.

THE GREAT DEBATE

6

Given time, reason is usually the master of unreason. Facts have a way of re-presenting themselves to the intellect until they win acceptance. Just as surely as the persistent ocean grinds away at the stubborn cliffs on all its shores, so does the tide of human reason wear away at the towers of irrationality in both East and West. But it takes time, and time may be what we have precious little of in this dawn of a nuclear age.

Oceans do their work best when great storms are raging. So too are human institutions leveled, changed, and rebuilt most rapidly when popular movements of irresistible urgency are sweeping the globe. The industrial revolution was such a movement; anticolonialism is another; they are both still under way. Today the people need to raise their voices in yet another debate—on the question of survival itself. This issue has been forced upon us by developments in nuclear physics. Prior to the nuclear age, human beings simply did not have the means whereby they could destroy all life on this planet and even the planet itself; now they do have the means. Physicists admit that there is no scientific or technological reason why devices capable of accomplishing these things cannot be built. Given this fact, will anyone deny that how to control this power must be the Great Debate of our time—indeed, of all human time?

Yet so far this debate has been carried on in muted tones and mainly by a few people in high places, even though the choices made affect the lives and fortunes of all people. Why should this be so? There are many reasons, of course. There is the inertia of tradition: people persist in casting the problems of today into the mold of yesterday. There is the dependence upon symbols of authority: most people prefer to let the "Great White Father" worry about it rather than complicating their own lives. There is what we have called the Neanderthal mentality: pacifistic solutions go against every Neanderthalic fiber. But most important, I think, is the fatalistic sense of the inevitability of war, and this comes from the lack of any acceptable alternative, as most people see it. Caught in the apparent dilemma between surrender to World Communism or death in a nuclear war, these people have just simply stopped thinking about it. Should decisions which affect not only our way of life but also our very lives be allowed to pass by default? If you say "no," then I urge you to join in the Great Debate.

ASSUMPTIONS OF GRIT

Graduated Reciprocation in Tension-reduction, as an approach to international relations in a nuclear age, is based upon the assumption that the problems we face are primarily matters of human nature and human relationships. It therefore seeks solutions in the laws of human thinking and behaving. It assumes that the Soviet people *and* their leaders are more like us than like the bogey men our psycho-logic creates, and that therefore we can do business with them. It assumes that their prime motive, like ours, is security, not world domination, and that they are as eager as we are to avoid full-scale nuclear conflict. It assumes that the men in the Kremlin are susceptible to the pressures of public opinion, both from within and from without, since such pressures are an index of the success or failure of their system. It assumes that the Communists are as convinced that their way of life will win out in nonmilitary competition for men's minds as we are (or should be) that ours will. And finally, therefore, it assumes that the Russians would accept an unambiguous opportunity to help reduce world tensions—for reasons of good sense even if not for reasons of good will.

Are Our Policy Problems Primarily Matters of Human Nature and Relationships?

I do not believe that anyone, no matter how technologically oriented, would seriously argue that nuclear science inevitably leads to thermonuclear bombs. As a matter of fact, many scientists rationalize their contributions to weaponry on precisely the ground that they are not personally responsible for the military and political uses to which their discoveries are put. Yet most of these scientists are deeply concerned, as citizens, with the social effects of their knowledge. Even casual perusal of the *Bulletin of the Atomic Scientists* shows that most of the articles deal with questions of ethics, of politics, of economics, and even of psychology—but, unfortunately, often with little more than lay sophistication in these matters. The essential point is this: if our problems are primarily matters of human nature and human relationships, then we must search for solutions in these areas, even though the sciences involved may be relatively underdeveloped as compared with physics and chemistry. GRIT developed out of the intellectual framework of the social and behavioral sciences and draws its main support from the principles of these sciences.

Are the Soviets More Like Us than Bogey Men?

The social sciences have amassed a great deal of evidence for the essential similarity of peoples of different races and nationalities in many basic characteristics. For example, given roughly equal opportunities to learn, differences in measured intelligence are minimal, if indeed they exist at all. Basic principles governing learning seem to be common to all humans, as well as to most higher species, and problem-solving capacity appears to have been equitably distributed among the human races. Likewise humans appear to be similar in their capacities to experience emotions and in their basic modes of expressing them. Similarities extend to more subtle characteristics, too. In my own cross-cultural studies, I have been able to show that human groups as different as Americans, Greeks, Arabs, Japanese, and Navajo Indians use essentially the same basic qualitative dimensions in making meaningful judgments and even share subtle synesthetic tendencies and metaphors to a remarkable degree. True, people do speak different languages and create different cultures, yet beneath these more visible differences lies the mass of the common human iceberg.

But what about the Russians and the Chinese? There is certainly no reason to believe them deviant from the rest of humanity simply because they adhere to a Communist ideology. Basic modes of human thinking and behaving do not change in chameleon-like fashion as people shift from being our allies to being our enemies and vice versa. There are Russians of the same stock, and Chinese of the same stock, who are not Communist, along with those who are. Put in this bald fashion, my proposition of essential human identity may seem too obvious, but nevertheless, under the stresses of wars both "cold" and "hot," people tend to exaggerate differences and minimize similarities. As Erich Fromm has warned, we must not be deceived by the slogans of Communist ideology; the Soviet Union in its Khrushchevist stage is already far removed from Marxist Socialism, being more a kind of state capitalism than a revolutionary movement, and appropriately conservative.

I realize that one can point to what seems to be contrary evidence about the Communists: there were bloodbaths during the early days of their revolution and there have been some violent purges since then; there was the ruthless stamping down of resistance in Hungary; there are salt mines in Siberia; and there have been executions of men like Nagy. It is to be regretted that men can be inhumanly cruel to other men, but this is a potentiality in all of us. The Russians would point to the sadism and the cruelty of the Germans whom we are now rearming; they would claim that the Hungarian revolt was Capitalist-inspired; and they would ask about the beam in our own eye: our massacres of whole Indian villages, our use of atomic bombs against Japanese civilian centers, the racial violence going on right now in some of our cities. True, we have explanations for these things, but they are just as blind to our justifications as we are to theirs.

In a speech before the American Psychological Association,[1] Ralph K. White, an expert on Soviet psychology for the USIA, gave impressive evidence for the "mirror image" in American-Soviet relations. His statements were documented by quotations from leaders and experts on both sides. "Statistically [the mirror-image phenomenon] is represented by the fact that 45 per cent of the themes and subthemes on the American side have almost identically worded counterparts on the Soviet side, and another 32 per cent have counterparts that are similar if not identical." The six major mirror-image resemblances were these: (1) attributing aggressive intent to the other; (2) attributing peaceful intent to the self; (3) judging both self and other in terms of essentially the same criteria (truthfulness, unselfishness, material well-being, strength, unity, courage, etc.); (4) having a "blacktop" image of the other (it is the enemy *leaders* who are evil, not the people); (5) saying that we must not listen to the other because he always tells lies; (6) refusing to believe that the other side is motivated by fear of our side.

White also demonstrated that there are real differences in viewpoint between the Russians and ourselves. For one thing, we have quite different conceptions of "democracy": they give lip service to government of and for the people, but seldom mention the essential individual freedoms that give meaning to this conception. For another, we have different attitudes toward deception: they accept rational and skillful deception in the interest of Communism as moral, whereas for us deception is always immoral (and we become outraged when our own transgressions are pointed out to us). We have a higher regard for facts than they do: for us, facts are more sacred than theories, political as well as scientific, while for them the reverse seems to hold true. And finally, according to White, the Russians cling to a warm

---

[1] Ralph K. White, "Misconceptions in Soviet and American Images," American Psychological Association convention, New York, September, 1961.

feeling of friendliness toward the American people which we do not seem to reciprocate—a point well worth keeping in mind.

What, then, should we conclude about the Russian bogey? It would be unrealistic, and in fact downright dangerous, to discount the real differences between the Soviets and ourselves, particularly those concerning the values and rights of individual human beings which stem from our ideological conflict. But our problem is one of being *objective*, of sifting the real and significant differences from those created in the workings of our own minds. I am sure that the Russian bogey has been grossly overdrawn in the dynamics of our own psycho-logic, as has their image of us, particularly by those on both sides who are emotionally incapable of distinguishing between their present opponent and German Nazism. In other words, I think that *the mutual bogey man images can be cut down to more realistic size and shape.* By doing so, we will free ourselves for more rational and flexible dealings with the opponent. This is not easy to do, as any psychiatrist knows: a major emotional investment has been made in these distortions, they are maintained by the mechanism of the self-fulfilling prophecy, and people avoid exposing themselves to contrary information; but do it we must to escape from the present psychological dilemma.

Is the Prime Soviet Motive Security and Do They Want to Avoid Nuclear War as Much as We Do?

It is extraordinarily difficult for us to believe that anyone, including the Russians, should really be afraid of us. This is because we project our own self-image of peaceful intent upon others and assume that they must see us the same way we see ourselves. Recent travelers to the Soviet Union, including some social scientists whom I know personally,[2] report that this definitely is not the case. "Why do you Americans want war?" our informal ambassadors are asked. And when they reply that we most definitely do not want war, the Russians ask, "Then why do your leaders prepare for it? Why do they ring us about with missile bases?" When our travelers ask them why *they* are building up nuclear

---

[2] See Urie Bronfenbrenner, "The Mirror Image in Soviet-American Relations. A Social Psychologist's Report," Cornell University, 1961 (privately distributed).

weapons for long-range attack and why they broke the test ban, they reply that we leave them no choice. "We must defend ourselves."

I believe that we must accept these protestations of good faith as genuine. They blame their warlike behavior on us just as we blame ours on them. Their prime motive, just as ours, is a somewhat frantic search for security against what is perceived as an overwhelming external threat. Explicit recognition and acceptance by both sides of the fact that the driving motive in international relations today is *reciprocal fear* would itself go a long way toward easing tensions. Both would become more sensitive to the threatening aspects of their own actions. But, you now ask, if we were to reduce threat, would not their other motive—world domination by Communism—become dominant? Yes, undoubtedly, much in the same sense that we are dedicated to the strengthening of the Free World and the irradication of Communism as a way of life. But the important thing is that the methods of waging this long-term conflict would be different and much less liable to eliminate both contenders.

Are the Russians as eager to avoid a "hot" nuclear war as we are? I would say that they are probably more so. Men who have been face to face with disaster are more wary about its repetition than those who have only heard about it. During World War II, as we noted in an earlier chapter, the Russian people experienced heavy bombing of their cities and lost some 20 million lives; the American people have never had an experience like this. A colleague of mine who specializes in studies of the mass media as a means of understanding popular culture has visited Russia and other countries in Eastern Europe, and he reports being impressed with the emphasis on peace themes in the media there, as compared with our own emphasis on more aggressive themes. It is also clear that Khrushchev has definitely scrapped the Marxist-Leninist notion of the inevitability of war with the Capitalist nations; according to reports, he is sensitive to the need to meet growing consumer demands, to the popular opposition to war, and to the uncertainty of what might happen in the satellite states in case of overt hostilities.

There are, of course, case-hardened statesmen who believe that our conflict with Communism lies primarily in disagreement over who is to control the great and increasingly important un-committed areas of the world, rather than in ideological conflict per se. There are also many well-disciplined political scientists who will claim that the underlying source of international tension today is still what it has always been—the struggle for power. In this struggle, they will argue, weapons are simply instruments for changing the balance of power, whether the weapons be clubs or nuclear warheads. I think this interpretation has become untenable in the nuclear age. Even though the behavior of na-tions in the past has often conformed to this image, I suspect that even then the Neanderthalic bluster masked a deeper anx-iety. Today mutual insecurity rather than the struggle for power has become the major source of international tensions; elites in both East and West now seem to accept national security as their primary responsibility and base their decisions upon it.

Are the Men in the Kremlin Susceptible to Pressures of Public Opinion?

We are accustomed to contrasting the responsiveness of our leaders to the will of the people with the irresponsibility of the Soviet leadership. There is certainly a real difference here, but we exaggerate it. We are also accustomed to thinking about the average man in the Communist state as being kept in ignorance of what is going on in the outside world, and this, too, is correct but exaggerated. Ithiel Pool, a specialist on international com-munications,[3] has pointed to the vital significance the Soviet leaders attribute to public opinion (polls of a sort have recently been instituted in Russia); he also emphasizes the fact that Western ideas continually penetrate the Soviet walls, through highly effective word-of-mouth channels and through the moni-toring operations of the elite. Recently we have seen further breaks in this communications barrier—the full publication of an interview with President Kennedy in *Izvestia*, arrangements for joint Russo-American filming of movies, and at least plans for an exchange of television appearances by Khrushchev and Kennedy in each other's countries. It is extremely doubtful if the Russian leaders could prevent dissemination of news about GRIT to their people.

---

[3] Ithiel Pool, "Public Opinion and the Control of Armaments," in G. Holton (ed.), *Arms Control*, special issue of *Daedalus*, Fall, 1960, pp. 984-999.

As to developments in world opinion outside the Soviet Union, it seems that the Russian leaders, at least, are as keenly aware of them and alert to them as we are. They have developed as effective feedback systems ("intelligence") as we have. If strong moral pressures were to develop in neutral nations, we could be sure that the Soviets would be aware of it and react to it in some way. It has been claimed that the resumption of testing by the Russians shows they have no regard for world opinion; what it more likely shows is that they have other motives, particularly fear and insecurity, which override their concern for world opinion. Does our own resumption of testing, equally in the face of world opinion and, indeed, much home opinion, mean that our leaders are completely insensitive to what others think? Both sides are eager to win the good will and support of other nations, but this is neither their exclusive nor dominant motive.

Are the Communists as Convinced that Their Way of Life Will Win Out in Nonmilitary Competition as We Are that Ours Will?

Here the answer seems to be that the Soviets are *more* confident of their ultimate success than we are of ours. Reports of foreign observers and travelers again are almost unanimous on this matter. The Russian man-on-the-street is extraordinarily conscious and proud of the material progress Communism has made in the past few decades; he sees it as a "leap ahead," and when compared with his state some 40 years ago, it is. However, he is equally conscious and envious of the contrast in material wealth and well-being that still exists between his life and that of most Americans, and he is determined to "bury us" in the race for material well-being. In a somewhat less flamboyant way, the Russian of today is imbued with much the same spirit as the American of the period of Westward expansion. He likes to think that his version of everything is the biggest and best, and he is a bottomless well for praise, as most visitors soon discover. We should give him praise where praise is due; it may be hard on our psycho-logic, but it does wonders for international relations.

What about ourselves? Why are we not equally confident that our way of life would win out in peaceful competition for men's minds? For one thing, being the wealthiest nation on earth, we have adopted a "fat cat" attitude, taking what we have for granted and mainly trying to keep it. For another thing, in our rather recently acquired role as defenders of the status quo, we seem to have lost sight of the fact that our way of life is itself a major revolution in the relation between individual and state. Furthermore, in keeping with psycho-logic, we have attributed to Communism a degree of power and omnipotence that justifies our being so afraid of it. Nevertheless, I find it hard to understand why we Americans are so insecure about our own principles—so insecure that we are afraid to expose our young people to "alien" ideas, so insecure that we feel threatened by nonconformity, so insecure that we support "Un-American Activities Committees."

Quite some time ago, and without obvious implementation, Khrushchev announced the doctrine of "peaceful coexistence." By this was meant "peace" as far as military means are concerned but "war" as far as social, political, and economic means are concerned. Khrushchev has stuck to this position, despite the Paris Summit debacle and despite strong pressures from both the Stalinists and the Chinese Communists. This seems to be testimony as to where Khrushchev himself stands and as to the state of public and elite opinion in much of Russia. It is a good thing for us that the Communists do have this self-confidence in the superiority of their way of life and believe that they will win out in nonmilitary competition—as long as we are equally convinced that they are wrong. Mutual self-confidence permits both sides to forgo a military resolution. I, for one, am convinced that our way of life is much closer than Communism to the "natural" state toward which human beings tend as they acquire economic sufficiency, political security, and intellectual opportunity. But to convince others of this requires demonstration in deeds rather than suffocation in words.

Would the Soviets Accept an Unambiguous Opportunity to Help Reduce World Tensions?

This, obviously, is the 64,000-dollar question, but today one should put the sum in billions. I believe that all of the arguments presented so far support the conclusion that they would join us in a controlled and calculated march toward a more peaceful world. The similarities between us are certainly much greater than the differences we stress, as we will realize when we take off our psycho-logical spectacles and take an objective look at the world. Their perceptions of the present situation and their reactions to it are therefore likely to be much more like our own than we would now predict. And certainly they would welcome a way out as much as we would. Of course we can use their intense concern over nuclear war to justify a "get even tougher" policy, but we should have learned by now that this merely drives them all the harder to outrace us in armaments; or we can use this concern on their part to justify a gamble that they would reciprocate in an open, unambiguous policy of tension-reduction and control.

We should also keep in mind the fact that the Russian Communists are aware of the growing power of the Chinese Communists, and they undoubtedly would like to be in a better position to meet it over the coming decades. The Soviet Union shares an extended boundary with burgeoning China, and minor conflicts over territory have already taken place. These two centers of Communist power also feel themselves to be in competition for leadership in the minds of the underdeveloped countries; the situations in North Korea, in the Congo, and in Cuba (where the Chinese recently worked out a 60-million-dollar loan agreement) are cases in point. We note further that the Soviet Union has not been particularly eager to put nuclear weapons in the hands of the Chinese or to assist them in developing their own. Apparently the Russians can read the writing on the Great Wall. Again, we can use this friction within the Communist bloc to justify further increasing the pressure, in the hope the bloc will split (actually this pressure is one of the few forces welding it); or we can use it as an inducement to the Soviets to reciprocate in reducing world tensions, so that both together can then act to bring Red China gradually into the world community.

It is precisely because our policy must be *unambiguous* that programs of graduated unilateral initiative are recommended. Atlhough bilateral agreements—particularly treaties formally signed and ratified—may be more explicit and binding once attained, the problem is in the difficulty of attainment under present conditions of mutual suspicion and distrust. GRIT would enable us to create conviction as to our intentions through deeds rather than words and would enable us to generate mounting pressure toward reciprocation. This approach is not to be considered an alternative to negotiation; rather, it should be viewed as a "psychological primer," as a means of reversing the arms race and reducing world tensions to a level where serious negotiations leading toward a stabilized peaceful world could be successfully undertaken.

ROARS FROM NEANDERTHALAND

There are many objections to any unilateral, nonaggressive policy of this sort. It will be well to anticipate these objections and try to answer them as part of the Great Debate. In the course of writing and lecturing on GRIT I have had the benefit of many critical discussions with colleagues in various fields, as well as critical questions from audiences. I think this has helped me press my own ideas into harder and clearer form. Objections to GRIT tend to fall into two general categories. First, there are more emotional objections, grounded in the dynamics of what I have called the Neanderthal mentality, but they are nonetheless effective because they flow more from emotion than sweet reason. Then there are rational and subtle objections, based upon strategic and tactical considerations. We shall hear the roars first and the queries second.

Communists *Are* Bogey Men

The most deep-seated emotional resistance to GRIT stems from the bogey man conception of the enemy. The tendency to see the world in terms of a simple bipolar conflict between Good and Evil is deeply ingrained in human thinking, and the particular Free World/Communism version of it has been drilled into us for many years now. Not only are there strong psychological resistances to restructuring one's world view in any case, but in the present case—where the two groups in conflict have mirror images of the world—almost everything seen, read, and heard seems to confirm the dominant view. In other words, each side, itself behaving in terms of a hostile enemy, continually creates the image of an equally hostile enemy in the eyes of its opponent. Taking the bogey man conception of the Soviets at face value, many people will argue that *any* unilateral action on our part designed to reduce tensions must be interpreted by THEM as a sign of weakness and, given their despotic drive toward World Communism, will only encourage them to encroach further on the Free World.

As an illustration of the intensity with which the bogey man conception is held, observe the immediate aftermath of Ralph K. White's address on the mirror-image phenomenon before the American Psychological Association on Monday, September 4, 1961. On Friday, September 8, the opening paragraph of a news release read as follows: "The summary dismissal of a top USIA expert on Russia and a Congressional investigation of the agency itself was demanded today in a Senate speech by Senator Thomas J. Dodd." The Senator did not question the validity of our image of THEM, but he objected most violently to the evidence that the Russian people hold much the same image of US—that they see us as warlike and their own government as peaceful, that they think most of what we tell them is lies, that they arm themselves because of fear of us, and so forth. To the contrary, the Senator contended, the Soviet people are "seething with discontent and hostility toward their Communist rulers." Apart from the question of substantive fact (and White's paper was amply documented), there is here the very serious and disturbing question of whether a public official who is also a trained scientist can report objective facts when they happen to run counter to the dogma of the day. If he cannot—as is often the case in the Soviet Union—then the prospects for rational and objective policy are dim indeed.

Everything I know about the social and behavioral sciences convinces me that the Russian bogey has been overdrawn in the workings of our own mental dynamics. I have emphasized its nature and development just because it is such an important source of resistance to rational policy decisions. But now let us assume that I am wrong—that the men in the Kremlin are in truth bogeys of the dimensions usually portrayed; does this rule out GRIT? I do not think so. It is a means of applying pressure toward certain kinds of international behavior that satisfy mutual self-interest, and we could therefore expect the Soviets to cooperate for reasons of good sense, quite apart from good will. Furthermore, it is a learning process; we might expect the Soviet bogey to be modified in course. And even if they proved to be inherently and unalterably evil, the very gradualness of GRIT and the fact that we retain our ultimate capacity to retaliate means that we could make sure that this was their nature without shifting the present balance of power to any significant degree.

Surely it would be a tragedy, a cause for cosmic irony, if two of the most civilized nations on earth were to drive each other to their mutual destruction because of their mutually threatening conceptions of each other—without ever testing the validity of these conceptions. GRIT offers us a means of making such a test. The test might prove that our conceptions have, indeed, been badly distorted by the mechanisms of cold war thinking. The test might, it is true, prove our conceptions largely correct. But, at the very least, we would have made a sincere effort to determine their real intentions, and the limited risk involved would be more than offset by the gain in favorable world opinion.

GRIT Is a Communist-inspired Trojan Horse

Psycho-logic lubricates the groove along which we slide those who disagree with us into the Communist camp, particularly when the disagreement involves matters of national security. My argument that GRIT is a strategy designed to get us out of a serious dilemma and, in the long run, to preserve our way of life will be incomprehensible to those whose psycho-logic is completely rigid. The fact that I have criticized some of the actions and policies of this country—and worse, have questioned the validity of the Soviet bogey and even justified some of his actions —runs contrary to the double standard of national morality. At the very least, anyone who proposes such a scheme must have fallen for the Communist line, such people will say, must be trying to "soften us up," and therefore is working for Communism, whether wittingly or unwittingly.

But disagreement with X does not necessarily imply agreement with Y. Psycho-logic yields emotional consistency, not logical consistency. Even such a staunch opponent of Communism as Mr. J. Edgar Hoover has repeatedly pointed out that dissent from popularly or even officially held views does not necessarily imply pro-Communism, even where the dissent may happen to parallel some Communist line. To follow the dictates of psycho-logic to their extreme means that we cut ourselves off from all sources of healthy self-criticism, and this is just what we need in times of national stress. As a matter of fact, my argument is that our way of life flourishes in times of relative peace, and therefore—if anything—GRIT would be a Trojan horse in the Communist camp.

This Is the Coward's Way

More people may see this approach to international relations as cowardly and therefore entirely distasteful. They would interpret GRIT as a proposal that we surrender without a fight and begin a kind of moral disarmament. There appear to be three main sources of this objection. First, these people do not distinguish GRIT from the kind of abject and complete disarmament proposed by many pacifist groups, except that here we disarm ourselves "on the installment plan," as one of my critics once put it. Second, personifying international relations, they believe that when a strong man makes any conciliatory gesture it must be a sign of weakness. Third, having denied the real nature of nuclear weapons, they still see war as a challenge to manhood and heroism.

If there was little opportunity for personal heroism and glory in World War II as compared with the individual combats of the days of King Arthur, it will be completely lacking in World War III, when missiles launched from thousands of miles away destroy whole cities of cowering civilians. On the matter of conciliatory gestures, it should be realized that there is an essential difference between prudence and appeasement: if a strong man makes a conciliatory move on his own initiative, it is a sign of his strength and confidence; if he made the same move under threat and pressure from an opponent, then we could legitimately call it "appeasement." Men who rely on their brains rather than their brawn are not necessarily cowards, particularly when brawn is peculiarly susceptible to the effects of radiation. Finally, people who would view this as the coward's way have failed to appreciate two critical characteristics of GRIT: one, the fact that we retain our capacity to retaliate with nuclear weapons should we be attacked, as well as the capacity to meet limited aggression with limited resistance; two, the fact that we regulate our own steps in terms of the reciprocation obtained or not obtained from the opponent. A policy that employs unilateral initiatives in tension control as a deliberate means of inducing an opponent to reciprocate can hardly be called "surrender."

It Is an Idealist Phantasy

Here we have one of the most pernicious sources of resistance to GRIT or any other tension-reducing policy. Washington today divides itself rather neatly into those who consider themselves to be "hardheaded realists" and those whom *they* consider to be "softheaded idealists." The hardheads differ from the more naive adherents to the Russian bogey conception in that they see *both* sides as realistically pursuing their self-interest in the traditional game of international power politics. They would say that to weaken one's own position in any way in the present situation is as softheaded as it is softhearted. The only thing that the Communists understand is raw force, and it is with this that we must present them. These hard-nosed men seldom look around the corner into the future to see where all this is leading us; they are, after all, practical men concerned with the problems of today.

However, what seems realistic within one time-bound frame of reference may prove to be highly unrealistic in the broader scheme of things. What we call "realistic" usually depends upon what is habitual, what is familiar, and upon immediate goals. Thus it is realistic to concentrate on earning a living, getting one's children through school, and getting a little fun out of life, but it is idealistic to concentrate upon the world of the future. It is realistic to demand more weapons when faced with external threat and idealistic to worry about where it is all leading. But novel situations demand new definitions of what is realistic, and now we are certainly in a novel situation. Who are the real idealists today? I think they are the physicists who honestly believe that stabilized deterrence can be continued indefinitely while they go on playing with their nuclear toys; I think they are the generals who honestly believe that the men behind the nuclear weapons are completely rational and will behave like so many computers; I think they are the statesmen who honestly believe that the Russians will back down if we just keep "getting tougher." If we have not backed down to their threats in the past, why should we expect them to back down to ours?

The "hard" *vs.* "soft" continuum is more a matter of personality than of political realism or idealism. You will find hard-nosed thinkers and actors on both sides of the policy spectrum; they differ primarily in their basic assumptions about the enemy, about ourselves, and about the nature of the world we are now living in. But the nature of the real world has a way of forcing itself upon alert minds, no matter where they place themselves on the policy spectrum. If I am right in my own observations of the policy scene, then over the past few years there has been a gradual shift from policy extremes in toward what may become a common viewpoint. The nature of man and the realities of the system of competing national sovereignties have been forcing peace-oriented people toward more feasible proposals. The nature of the nuclear age and the realities of a system of unstable deterrence have been forcing war-oriented people toward proposals of tension control through arms control. GRIT contains elements of both; its aim is a more peaceful world and its method is one of tension control.

QUERIES FROM HOMO SAPIENS

The objections to unilateral initiative in tension-reduction we have been considering—that it is soft on Communism, cowardly, idealistic, and fails to take into account the true nature of our enemy—are important just because they are based largely on emotion. As such, they are difficult to reach by means of rational argument. But there are also objections that have been raised to this approach on grounds other than its emotional unpopularity. These concern its feasibility, in terms of both internal and external sources of resistance, whether it meets the many complex requirements of foreign policy, and its strategic and tactical aspects. These objections can be met in reasonable debate, and perhaps satisfied.

Would the Emotional Resistances Just Described Prevent Acceptance of GRIT?

Many who might agree with the general logic of my proposal may nevertheless conclude regretfully that it just simply is not feasible, given the intense emotional resistances to any conciliatory approach. Existing public beliefs and attitudes, they would say, make it likely that even if such a policy were adopted and sponsored by thoughtful and courageous leaders, both it and they would be rejected by the vast majority of people in this country. The outcries of "appeasement" and "surrender" would become louder with every unilateral initiative designed to reduce tensions and, in effect, would result in more dangerous tensions than we have right now. This is a rational objection and it must be met.

First, I would say that unpopular causes have been won before, and in this case I think the tide of reason is on our side. But it is not easy, and equal courage and dedication would be demanded of policy-makers, people in the mass media, and community opinion leaders in business, church, and school. Attitudes and beliefs can be changed. During the period when Russia became our ally and defended Stalingrad, some of my own research at the time showed that we came not only to think of them as much more *kind, noble,* and *fair,* but even as more *Christian!* And this all happened within the span of a few months. It is in a way fortunate that most Americans have such weakly anchored attitudes about foreign affairs, because weakly held attitudes are more susceptible to change. However, changes in public attitudes and beliefs depend more upon events and their interpretation than upon conviction through argument. Here, again, the fact that GRIT involves deeds more than mere words becomes important. Many events occur inadvertently in our complex world, but events can also be produced and interpreted by leaders whose opinions count.

Despite the unilateral initiative that characterizes GRIT, it should be apparent that the two parties in conflict are actually dependent on each other for its success. On each side there are competing factions spread over the spectrum of policy alternatives; just as we have our Birchers, so does the Soviet Union have its Stalinists. If our President, exercising administrative initiative, were to announce and execute a carefully planned series of tension-reducing moves, opposition groups in the United States government, in the mass media, and in the public at large would become increasingly critical. The only way to damp this opposition and keep the policy moving, in the long run, would be to receive reciprocation from the opponent. I am sure that much the same thing would be true for Soviet initiation. Thus, in a real sense, *successful reversal of the arms race requires implicit cooperation from enlightened leadership on both sides.* The leadership of the nation initiating such a policy would be risking its position to some extent, and the opposition leadership could assist in the demise by withholding reciprocation; but in doing so the opponent should be fully aware of the fact that he is strengthening forces in the other nation more violently antagonistic to him and more likely to act inflexibly and irrationally in future relations.

Thus it is to the advantage of each side to be on the alert for tension-reducing probes from the other and to be prepared to reciprocate in ways that will allow the process to continue. In recent history we have seen what appear to be tentative moves in this direction. In congratulating the United States on the successful orbiting of Colonel Glenn, for example, Chairman Khrushchev proposed that the United States and the U.S.S.R. cooperate in the further exploration of space; President Kennedy promptly accepted in principle, and the means of implementing this joint effort are being worked out at the time of this writing.

Also implicit in the relations between nation states is the problem of communicating simultaneously to many audiences. When President Kennedy announced that the United States planned to resume atmospheric testing of nuclear devices in April or May of 1962, he was speaking simultaneously to the military-industrial-scientific complex which produces nuclear weapons, to members of SANE and Mothers for Peace, to both our allies and to neutrals, *and* to the Soviet Union. One would like to believe that the real message beamed to Khrushchev was that if the United States and the U.S.S.R. could reach agreements on a test ban with adequate inspection in March of 1962, the new aerial tests would be canceled—and that the more aggressive "ultimatum" tone was primarily for home consumption. Perhaps we need special interpreters in each capital to unwrap the intended international message from its nationalistic packaging!

Is It Possible for the United States to Have Disarmament Without Also Having a Disastrous Depression?

Many people in this country express the fear that large-scale disarmament, including the cessation of weapons production, would create a depression far worse than that of 1929, and this in turn would create the conditions for a take-over of the country by internal Communism. They point to the immense investment of money, material, and people in the arms race, to the degree to which the skills, knowledge, prestige, and financial rewards of people in the military, in science, and in industry have become oriented toward this activity, and to the way political influence has been exerted by this complex. It is interesting to note that this is exactly the Marxist-Leninist line; it says that the Capitalist system, by the very nature of its underlying profit motive, must have war as an outlet for its overproduction and underconsumption. It is also worth noting that whereas the Soviets appear to have changed their line—war with the Capitalists is no longer held to be inevitable—many Americans appear to have accepted this dogma.

Is economic depression a necessary consequence of disarmament by the United States? I have discussed this question with a number of economists who have studied this specific problem, and the consensus seems to be that there is nothing in economics per se that makes depression a necessary consequence of disarmament. There are many other demands into which the supplies of our capital and our productive energy could be put—into underwriting the economic development of the rest of the world, as Melman has proposed, into the development of our own underdeveloped areas at home, into much-needed support of our educational, health, and welfare programs, and so forth. Although the national government has done very little planning for readjustment to peace, which itself speaks for a lack of faith in achieving nonmilitary solutions, many defense industries have been making such plans, for example, to shift from producing radar and sonar surveillance systems into producing broadcasting equipment. There would also be retooling problems, both for equipment and for men. We should be preparing for such massive readjustments—otherwise we will be creating another self-fulfilling prophecy.

The real question seems to be not whether the American economy *could* make the transition from a war economy to a peace economy but whether it *would* make this transition. As we have seen, the public eagerly pays taxes for defense; what would be its motivation to pay taxes for government support of massive foreign aid in a peaceful world, for schools and highways, for health and public works? Again, the problem appears to be more psychological than economic: how to motivate people to support activities that do not seem to involve imminent life and death. Perhaps it would take the onset of a depression to generate support for such peacetime programs. But the planning should anticipate the event, if we are to avoid a major depression and its consequences. The gradualness of GRIT would be an advantage here: whereas abrupt and complete disarmament would almost certainly throw our economy into a tailspin, a gradual reduction in the atmosphere of tension would enliven government and private plans for transition, then reciprocal steps in economic and scientific areas would begin to divert our productive capacity and imagination, and finally successful agreements on major disarmament would find an economy already well under way with its retooling.

Would This Policy Amount to a Betrayal of Our Obligation to Defend the Free World?

It is true that in this bipolar world the United States is the main bulwark of democratic institutions, even though we are by no means consistent in upholding them. It is also true that the application of GRIT would mean taking steps that reduce our military support in some areas where Communism is now in delicate balance with more liberal political views. The question is whether this would necessarily imply defeat of our way of life in these areas—and this is also a sensible question.

Before we can say anything about "betrayal of our obligation" we must first say something about what "defending the Free World" really means. I think what it *should* mean is actions on our part that strengthen the internal security and stability of other nations, that serve to support the development of democratic institutions (even though we cannot expect full-blown models of our way of life to appear overnight), that serve to create mutual interdependencies between ourselves and these other nations, and that reduce their sense of external threat as well as our own. I believe that, in the long run, the underdeveloped countries will achieve the greatest security if we and the Russians help strengthen their economic and educational base, without worrying so much about their political color, and stop using them as pawns in our global, cold war chess game. Even if we were, against our own self-interest, to engage in continuous "brush-fire" wars about the perimeter of the Free World, one can reasonably ask in what sense this "defends" other nations. In the sparring of the two giants, it is the little countries on whose soils the skirmishes take place that suffer the most severe wounds.

The direct fact of the matter is that our own security in a nuclear age is coming to depend less and less upon alliances or upon territorial control. Alliances provide the illusion of security in numbers, but it is without substance in an age of intercontinental missiles. Just as we would not now lightly risk starting a full-scale nuclear war for some remote foreign objective, so is our own liability to attack becoming independent of geographical distance. Yet every time we commit ourselves to the military defense of some other country, we are literally sacrificing our own sovereignty—and piecemeal, rather than to an international body like the United Nations. In situations like Berlin, the decision for peace or war can too easily be taken out of our hands. But here is the dilemma: how can we restrain the spread of Communism without taking this risk?

There is no simple answer to this, of course. One part of it is to shift our emphasis in foreign aid from military toward social, economic, and political strengthening; Communist infiltration and subversion have been most effective in countries where the existing governments were already rotten at the core and without deep-rooted support of their people. Another part of the answer lies in strengthening the peace-keeping machinery of the United Nations; this international body has already prevented escalation of limited conflicts in several areas. But the major part of the answer lies in reducing tensions between East and West throughout the world generally. By this means we can reduce the pressures on our opponents to "convert" their neighbors in the name of security. By this means, also, we can build interdependencies *between* East and West that serve as brakes to further aggression. The more dependent two groups are on each other, the less ready is either to disrupt the relation. These far-reaching changes cannot come about abruptly; they must be brought about gradually by the intelligent selection of our own initiatives in foreign affairs.

What About the Growing Menace of Red China?

It is true that the orientation of this book has been primarily toward United States–U.S.S.R. relations, with only occasional glances at the new Giant of the East. This has been equally true of American foreign policy. The reason in both cases, I think, is that as of this moment the Soviet Union is the only Communist nation with nuclear weapons and the means of their delivery. The *immediate* problem, therefore, is some kind of rapprochement with the Russians before we blow each other off the map. Given that, both Western nations would be in a better position to deal effectively with Communist China.

But here we find ourselves in new dilemmas. Not only because of the very nature of nuclear technology and weaponry, but also because of Soviet insistence, any negotiations for general and complete disarmament, with transfer of inspection and policing authority to some international body like the United Nations, must involve all nations—and particularly Communist China, with her fourth of the total population of the earth. Here, as we have seen, we run full tilt into a monstrous Sacred Cow of American foreign policy: we are unwilling even to recognize, to say nothing of negotiate with, Red China. We also stand in real psychological danger of building up an even more frightening Chinese bogey in our attempt to resolve differences with the Russian bogey. Given the present stage of development of Communism in China, along with her population pressure and her isolation from the world community, it is certain that once she has nuclear weapons she will be extraordinarily hard to deal with. It therefore behooves us to begin working on the problem now.

Everything that has been said about the application of GRIT vis-à-vis the Soviet Union in this chapter and the last applies with equal force to our future relations with Communist China, except that it will probably require more of it. The general principle of maintaining adequate security while continually applying intelligent pressure toward reciprocation in reducing tensions certainly holds. However, the thing that must be realized is that we are in a better position to apply GRIT to China *now,* from a position of relative military strength, than we will be later, when our military strength has been reduced absolutely by reciprocative action with the Soviets or relatively by the nuclear development of China itself. We therefore have a double imperative to circumvent this Sacred Cow: to make fundamental adjustments with the Soviet Union possible and to reduce tensions with Red China before that country comes of nuclear age. GRIT offers a way in which this could be done—carefully and gradually—and perhaps with minimal internal repercussions. It seems probable that once this approach had begun to work with respect to the Soviet Union, it would become more acceptable in the public mind for dealing with China.

GRIT Involves Too Much Risk?

This policy would involve some risk—indeed, the open and explicit acceptance of risk is essential if the opponent is to be induced to reciprocate—but here the risk is calculated and finely graduated in amount. Furthermore, we retain the initiative throughout and are able to slow down or accelerate the process as the situation requires. We also retain our capacity for nuclear retaliation, should the opponent make any gross aggressive response. I believe that such risk must be taken in the interest of our long-term security. As I have tried to show, our present policy certainly involves at least equal risk, and continuing the arms race will create even greater risk. *We must simply accept the fact that there is no policy, no alternative we can choose, that entails no risk.* The best we can do is to weigh the risks involved in different policy alternatives against the ultimate security to be achieved. GRIT balances limited risks extended over a long time-scale against at least the hope of ultimate survival and preservation of our way of life.

Is It Possible to Design Initiatives That Will Reduce Tensions Significantly Without Also Endangering Our Vital Interests?

A number of critics have pointed out what they see as a fatal flaw in the rationale of GRIT. Actions on our part that would be tolerable in terms of maintaining national security would be insignificant in tension-reducing impact and therefore would not serve to induce reciprocation from the opponent. Conversely, actions which might have a significant impact on world tensions would be so threatening to our own security that no government responsible for the safety of its people could undertake them. Thus, what sounds good in theory would prove to be unworkable in practice.

This argument stems, I think, from a tautly overextended definition of "our vital interests." It is possible to define vital interest in such a way that the slightest friendly gesture becomes a matter of giving aid and comfort to the enemy, that strategic withdrawal from a pebble in the Pacific becomes a major defeat, and that acceptance of imperfect inspection becomes an invitation to certain disaster. The dynamics of cold war thinking stimulate such a definition, particularly when decision-making is based on mere possibilities rather than actual probabilities. Our really vital interests are our biological survival and the preservation of our way of life, and our deterrent capacity provides at least temporary protection of the former, if not the latter. We actually have a great deal of freedom in which to operate if we accept a reasonable definition of our vital interests, *provided* that we succeed in obtaining reciprocations from the opponent.

Another important point that needs to be re-emphasized here is the fact that there is no perfect correlation between the psychological tension-reducing impact of actions and their military significance. The course of recent Soviet-American relations is strewn with evidence of this. Prospects for the Vienna talks between Kennedy and Khrushchev damped tensions without changing one whit the military situation; the same holds for the recent exchange of our U-2 pilot for a Soviet spy. Construction of the wall in Berlin increased tensions considerably, without really affecting the military situation; the same holds for demands by the East Germans for exclusive use of certain air corridors to Berlin. Cooperative efforts in the further exploration of space, particularly if they were well publicized, could have great and continuing psychological impact—again, without influencing the actual military balance in any significant way. GRIT is a way of creating and maintaining psychological pressures toward reciprocative actions which, when obtained, serve to reduce tensions and make subsequent, more significant steps easier to take by both sides. Working first on the tension atmosphere, one can gradually move in toward the more critical and significant areas of arms control and disarmament.

Would GRIT Destroy the Credibility of Our Deterrent?

Even though the policy we are considering involves carefully graduated steps, and even though we retain during the process our capacity for intolerable retaliation, it is nevertheless true that the steps are designed to be tension-reducing and are announced as such. In a situation where our defense is based on the opponent's fear of retaliation, it is necessary for us to maintain his fear at a sufficiently high level, otherwise he will not be deterred. Cooperative and conciliatory moves on our part would lead him to doubt the firmness of our resolve actually to use our nuclear weapons if provoked. Thus GRIT, by its very nature, would destroy the credibility of our deterrent and invite the attack our nuclear deterrent is designed to prevent. On the surface this is a very compelling argument, but we need to dig beneath the surface.

In the first place, we must realize that there are two quite different kinds of behavior we wish to deter. *Behavior Type I: all-out nuclear attack on our heartland.* We clearly must deter the opponent from launching a surprise first strike against our cities and retaliatory sites, whether for preventive or pre-emptive purposes, by making our nuclear retaliation so certain and devastating that this course becomes untenable. Note that this kind of deterrence assumes only the credibility of our retaliatory second strike. *Behavior Type II: nonnuclear encroachments along the perimeter of the Free World.* We would like to deter the opponent from undertaking limited aggression anywhere along the far-flung boundary that divides East and West, whether it takes the form of ground attack in Europe or guerrilla action in Southeast Asia. Some military strategists believe that we must rely on the threat of nuclear attack to deter such encroachments, because the Soviet and Chinese conventional forces outweigh our own. Note that this kind of deterrence requires credibility that we will use our nuclear weapons for a first strike if sufficiently provoked.

In the second place, we must distinguish between two quite different kinds of credibility.[4] *Credibility Type A: the opponent's belief that we will attack if sufficiently provoked, but will not attack otherwise.* This is like the deterrence provided by rules of law or by the control of a wise parent over his child. The effective policeman or father creates an image of rational determination to uphold the rules; if provoked by failure to obey the rules, he will punish, but he certainly will not attack wantonly and in fact will be friendly and cooperative as long as the rules are followed. *Credibility Type B: the opponent's belief that we are liable to*

[4] I am grateful to Marc Pilisuk of the Mental Health Research Institute, University of Michigan, for giving me this insight, in a paper titled "The Hostile Enemy: A Factor in Credible Deterrence," 1961 (privately distributed).

attack even if not provoked. This is like the unstable kind of deterrence that operates between rival street gangs. By continuous threats and name-calling, the members of each gang create in the eyes of the other the image of an implacably hostile enemy —an enemy filled with hate and bent on his complete obliteration if any opportunity is given.

It should be obvious that Credibility Type B (we are out to get you in one way or another) used as a means of deterring Behavior Type II (any provocation anywhere in the world) creates an extremely dangerous and volatile situation. It is an open invitation to preventive or pre-emptive attack. Yet this is precisely the kind of deterrent posture toward which all the dynamics of Neanderthal thinking drive us: to create by our threats and name-calling the image of an unalterably hostile and irrationally unpredictable enemy who is always liable to make a first strike. Of course, this hostile-enemy image is reciprocal and therefore generates a vicious cycle.

Credibility Type A (firm but not hostile) is quite sufficient to deter Behavior Type I (all-out nuclear attack on our heartland). Surely the Soviet leaders are not so naive or irrational as to doubt that we would retaliate with everything we had following a nuclear attack on the United States. It seems clear, then, that our rational course should be to use Credibility Type A as a means of deterring Behavior Type I (preventive or pre-emptive attack) and rely upon conventional means to deter the nibbling process.

How does one create in his opponent's eyes the image of a determined but not hostile enemy? GRIT is designed to accomplish precisely this. By explicitly retaining our nuclear retaliatory capacity and meeting encroachments with pinpointed resistance, we create and maintain the image of firm resolve to retaliate if sufficiently provoked; yet by consistently taking the initiative with moves designed to reduce and control world tensions, we gradually create and maintain the parallel image of peaceful intent and lack of implacable hostility.

Is There Ever Good Reason to Increase Tensions?

I have been emphasizing the tension-reduction side of GRIT because I believe that the arms race is already getting out of hand and tensions are dangerously high. But the broadest conception is one of *tension control*. If you glance back at the figure on page 60, you will note that the optimum level of tension, in terms of behavioral flexibility and creativity, is not zero; under this condition the organism simply sleeps. Nations, too, need an adequate degree of energizing, from both internal and external competition, from demands for better standards of living, from being faced with serious problems (for example, control of the population explosion), and so forth. And often, in order to get a nation (or any other human group) to tackle a problem that demands maximum flexibility and creativity, it is necessary to raise tension levels.

The same rules presumably apply to relations between nations. In order to get a backward people ego-involved in their own economic and cultural development, rather than passively accepting spoon-feeding of aid as long as it is given, it may be necessary to induce tensions in a carefully designed fashion. For example, we might make tiny transistor radios easily available to the population and generate new felt needs by advertising techniques. In general, there is no reason to think that sources of adequate tension level would be lacking in a relatively disarmed world engaged in "peaceful competition," or that they could not be deliberately generated as required.

A number of experts on Russian strategy have claimed that the Soviet high command deliberately applies Pavlovian conditioning techniques to manipulate the United States. In particular, they point to the use of unpredictable increase and then decrease of tension as a means of keeping us "off balance." As far as the political use of conditioning and other behavioral science techniques is concerned, this may be true (though I doubt it). But it would be quite false to assume that Soviet scientists are further along in the development of "psychological warfare" (or "peace-fare") techniques than American scientists. These techniques include such things as persuasion and immunization to persuasion, tension manipulation, producing discrimination conflicts, and both producing and resolving cognitive stress. Comparison of Russian and American psychological literature in this area suggests that, if anything, the reverse is the case. However, there is great resistance in this country to the deliberate use of social science techniques—as compared with the use of physical and biological science techniques—even for socially acceptable ends.

Occasional alternation of tension-decreasing and tension-increasing (or maintaining) actions may be an effective technique. We have a well-documented psychological phenomenon known as *intermittent reinforcement*. During the learning of some new form of behavior, one group of subjects (either human or subhuman) is rewarded every time the correct response is given, whereas the other group is rewarded only intermittently and unpredictably; when we now try to extinguish the new form of behavior in these two groups—by giving a long series of trials without *any* reward—we observe a surprising thing: the intermittently reinforced subjects persist in the new behavior much longer than the consistently reinforced subjects. In other words, the intermittent group has come to expect that reinforcement will not be forthcoming every time, so they can survive a longer "dry period" without extinguishing. In a complex world, filled with unpredictabilities both within and outside the nation, we could confidently expect that there would be "dry periods" even if both we and the Soviets were trying to apply GRIT consistently. Therefore it would behoove us to intersperse tension-reducing initiatives (and reciprocations to Russian initiations) with actions that merely maintain the status quo or even raise tensions somewhat. This would probably increase the chances of the policy's surviving occasional prolonged periods of tension.

Would the Soviets Accept Our Initiatives, and We Their Reciprocations, as Bona Fide?

Using my own arguments about the nature of cold war thinking, some critics have claimed that the Russians would almost certainly perceive our initiatives as attempts at deception. Therefore they would resist reciprocation for such a long period that public opinion in our own country would bring this policy to a shuddering halt. And even if we designed our initiatives in such a way as to induce their reciprocation early on the basis of self-interest, would Americans not be extremely distrustful of their reciprocations, both in terms of their intent and their significance? After all, if our government is unwilling to accept a test-ban agreement without ironclad inspection—not only of testing but even of preparations for testing—how could we expect it to trust the Communists in an open, uncontrolled process like GRIT?

I would argue, first, that our real protection against being taken advantage of in any serious way lies in our undiminished capacity for nuclear retaliation, and exactly the same safeguard exists for the opponent. This is why the deterrent is also a security base for taking limited risks. Second, and perhaps most important, unilateral *acts,* unlike mutual discussions, have the status of *fait accompli,* like the satellites circling our globe. We would certainly design our initiatives and invited reciprocations to be as unambiguous and susceptible to verification as possible, and we would include unilateral invitation to inspection wherever feasible. Finally, there is the cumulative impact of a diversified program of actions: argument over the motivation of the first, and even the second or third, would tend to be resolved by the execution of the next and the next after that.

As to our distrust of Soviet reciprocations, there is a principle of human behavior that seems relevant: Man A's interpretation of Man B's reaction to him depends to a considerable extent upon Man A's own prior behavior toward B. If American Man had already made an intentional conciliatory move toward Russian Man, he would be much more likely to perceive the Russian's reciprocation as bona fide than if it had come unsolicited. Furthermore, as pointed out in the previous chapter, reciprocations are more likely to appear as Soviet initiations, but once the process is under way, this makes little difference.

This raises the question of how such a reciprocating system is maintained. The arms race has its own self-generating dynamics: each increment in military strength by one side creates the threat-stimulus driving the other side to catch up and get ahead. But what about GRIT? Will it not, like a pendulum set in motion by one push, gradually lose its momentum and come to a halt without some external support? I think not. This kind of international system would also generate its own dynamics, but based on the rewarding effects of tension-reduction rather than the threatening effects of tension-induction. Each successful cycle of GRIT would make the next cycle somewhat easier to accomplish, until this form of international behavior became as familiar and traditional as an arms race is now.

But the problem is how to get this new kind of reciprocative system started—how to give the pendulum a sufficient nudge. I believe that, even granting the atmosphere of mutual distrust in which such a process must begin, both internal and external pressures would force the opponents into at least token reciprocations at the low-risk level with which GRIT would be initiated. And here another principle of human behavior becomes relevant: when people are constrained by a situation to keep on behaving in ways that are inconsistent with their actual attitudes, their attitudes tend to shift gradually into line with their manifest behavior. If they are required to keep on behaving *as if* they really trusted each other—when in fact they definitely do not— they will gradually come to trust each other more. I think the same principle applies to nations. If we could initiate a series of reciprocated tension-reducing acts and maintain them over a sufficiently long period, the basic psychological conditions that now prevent us from taking larger and more significant steps toward world peace would be eliminated.

What if the Communists Did Try to Take Advantage of Our Actions?

If the enemy were to try to take advantage of our conciliatory moves, would this not have the "boomerang effect" of further intensifying our bogey man conception of him? Here would be the self-fulfilling prophecy with a vengeance! Many people, as we have seen, are convinced that the Communists would interpret our initiatives as a sign of weakness and would therefore be encouraged to encroach. If this were to happen, not only would GRIT be abandoned abruptly by this country, but we would be thrown into such a state of anger and frustration that preemptive war on our part might well be risked. Of course, it is quite likely that the enemy would be aware of this potential reaction on our part, and to that extent inhibited.

The possibility of encroachment is the main risk we take with this policy. However, with carefully graduated steps the likelihood of disruptive encroachment is minimal in the early stages, and to the extent that reciprocations are obtained, the probabilities of "taking advantage" become even less as the policy continues. It becomes more clearly advantageous to both participants to avoid getting caught up in the arms race again. Even if encroachment did occur at some stage in the process, this could be turned to advantage if met firmly. As I pointed out in an earlier chapter, given our nuclear retaliatory capacity, any encroachment would almost certainly be tentative and probing in nature. Offering firm but pinpointed resistance in the area of encroachment, while continuing our policy flexibly in other areas, would be a convincing demonstration that GRIT is not the same thing as surrender. It should also be noted that most of our initiatives in the early phases (for example, personnel exchanges, reducing trade barriers, and the like) would be of a nonmilitary nature and not readily susceptible to encroachment.

Actually, I think the real danger would lie not so much in deliberate attempts by one side to take advantage of the other as in each side failing to interpret correctly the risks and benefits of particular moves *as perceived by the other*. What might be seen by the Soviets as a big concession in the area of inspection we might consider piddling in significance, and what we viewed as a major disengagement in Southeast Asia they might treat as simply restoring the status quo—and once again we are trapped in biased perceptions of the equable. A great deal of talking back and forth would be required to keep check on what is bothering each side and on how various moves are being interpreted. This puts a premium on preparation of our policy-makers in depth and breadth, as well as on maintaining multiple levels of communication. In practice, the gradual, self-monitoring nature of GRIT should provide ample room for mutual communication and adjustment.

I have met both roars and queries as best I can. Perhaps I have satisfied the reader. If not, I must now turn the tables and ask a question of my own. *What do you suggest as a way out?* I believe this is a fair question. If you agree that merely going along as we are, preaching peaceful intentions but practicing an arms race, involves great risk, if you agree that prospects for agreement on disarmament are not very bright, if you are not willing to accept the consequences of either preventive war or abject surrender—but you nevertheless find GRIT too risky—then what alternative do you propose? There may be additional alternatives. Others may come up with something better than what is offered here. If so, then it, too, should be injected into the Great Debate.

WHITHER MANKIND?

In the last analysis, we are merely human—nothing more and nothing less. We are creatures of habit, servants of our emotions, and victims of our own mental dynamics. But on occasion we have been known to rise above mere habit, control our emotions, and exercise our minds in the solution of problems of incredible complexity. The same species that is capable of lynching one of its fellows in blind hatred is also capable of discovering ways of healing his most ravaging afflictions. Here in the middle of the twentieth century, only a few thousand years past the beginning of our civilization, our species has come face to face with a crisis that will require all its ingenuity and humanity to resolve. Depending upon how we act today, we will be choosing our future —and choose we must, because time waits for no species.

A Glance at the Road Behind

Born on the wings of science and technology, the nuclear age poses a completely novel problem for humans, even though most of them do not realize it as yet. It strikes them at precisely the time when competitive nationalism as a form of political organization is at its crest. Mature nations reached their present positions of eminence through the exercise of international power politics, and young nations are busily emulating these models of success. So we find nations trying to solve this novel problem along strictly traditional lines, firmly believing this course to be realistic.

But novel situations usually demand novel solutions. What is novel about our situation today? The main thing is that never before in the history of this planet have so few actually had the power to destroy so many and so much with so little effort. Competent authorities assure us that soon Russia and the United States will have nuclear, biological, and chemical weapons capable of annihilating each other many times over. There is no technological reason why even one small nation could not develop a nuclear or biological device capable of destroying all life on the planet. Right now submarines are slipping into the depths of the Atlantic, each of them armed with destructive power equal to all that was delivered on Germany and Japan during World War II. But this is not the only novel thing about our age: airborne planes can span continents in hours; space vehicles will soon be able to reach the nearby planets in days; and messages can be sent from New York to Calcutta in less time than it took to type this paragraph.

The products of man's scientific genius can be used for his betterment as well as for his destruction. The same energy that is released abruptly from the atom as blast could be released gradually as industrial power; the same plane that carries a nuclear warhead could be carrying visitors from country to country; the same communication system that coordinates a military machine could integrate a world government. Why are these alternatives not obvious? It is because we are caught in a great cultural lag. Our facility with gadgets has far outstripped our capacity to understand and control ourselves, and the present generation is faced with the consequences of this imbalance. If we call some nations underdeveloped, then in truth we should admit that others, including our own, are overdeveloped.

This imbalance between technology and civilization presents us with many paradoxes. The Neanderthal within drives both sides to pile weapon upon weapon for defense against an implacably hostile enemy. Yet because nuclear weapons are primarily offensive and not defensive, neither side gains security. Rather than being freed by our military power to act forcefully in international situations, we find ourselves bound by our moral reluctance to use it and by our fear of having it used against us. We realize that disarmament must be achieved somehow, yet our distrusts and suspicions prevent even token successes at the negotiation table.

A hard, objective evaluation of our present policy—mutual deterrence through fear of mutual annihilation—reveals its flat inadequacy in terms of even minimal criteria. It obviously fails to eliminate the threat of nuclear war; indeed, the arms race has been reaching toward ever more fantastic means of destruction. Nor does it serve to support our democratic way of life; indeed, it promotes a callousness to the rights of individual citizens that supports totalitarianism at home as well as abroad. And it really is not feasible over the long haul. Only the most optimistic idealists among us (who consider themselves to be hard-nosed) deny the possibilities of accident, pooh-pooh the irrationalities of men, and conclude that ordinary mortals can go on indefinitely handling such power without making mistakes.

But in what direction, then, lies a course of positive initiative in policy? If traditional unilateral actions of a tension-inducing nature are prohibitively dangerous, if traditional bilateral negotiations for disarmament are foredoomed by the very tensions that promote them, and if radical unilateral disarmament as a means of reducing tensions is unacceptable because it runs headlong into the flowing tide of nationalism—whither mankind?

Back to the Caves or Out to the Stars?

In the forefront of those who believe that nuclear war of some kind is highly probable is Herman Kahn, for a long time expert adviser on military policy for the RAND Corporation.[5] He has made a coldly rational assessment of the proportions of our population we might lose under various types of attack and of the number of years it would take us to rebuild our civilization. He concludes that we should undertake a shelter program. On the face of it, this sounds like plain, ordinary common sense: if there is a reasonable likelihood of nuclear attack, then by all means we should try to protect ourselves. I would agree with Kahn's grim assessment of the probability of nuclear war if we keep on going as we have been, but I disagree with his prescription. Why? Fundamentally because I believe a retreat to the caves would push what is now only a probability of nuclear war toward inevitability, without in any way serving to solve the basic policy problem.

What are some of the arguments in favor of a shelter program? The basic one is simply that any kind of program would save some lives, and the more elaborate and expensive the program the greater the proportion of the population that would be saved. Some people talk in terms of "insurance"; if war does come, then at least we have some protection. Another argument is that the most likely types of attack would be either a massive blow aimed at our retaliatory sites (in which case fallout would be the main cause of death to civilians) or an accidental attack (in which case having our civilians protected would help us delay and investigate).

A more subtle, and debatable, argument has been that civilian defense is a kind of deterrence in itself; the smaller the number

---

[5] Herman Kahn, *On Thermonuclear War*, Princeton University Press, 1960.

of civilians they think they can kill, the less likely will the Soviets be to risk an attack, and hence they cannot use "nuclear blackmail" so easily. An even more subtle, and more debatable, argument goes like this: with our civilians safely tucked in shelters, *we* can use "nuclear blackmail" more effectively as an instrument of national policy; our threat to launch a nuclear attack if provoked in any way, for example, in Berlin, becomes more credible. Finally, some have argued that the whole social complex of shelter-building, including practice alerts and the dissemination of information about nuclear war, will make the public more aware of the danger and thus frighten them into trying to find other alternatives.

The most dangerous deception sometimes practiced in this debate is the assurance of safety for all or nearly all in the face of nuclear attack. This was typified by the September 15, 1961, issue of *Life* magazine, whose cover pictured a man in a "civilian fallout suit" (later admitted to be useless) and carried a headline claiming that "97 OUT OF 100 PEOPLE CAN BE SAVED." Even those scientists who generally support shelter-building make no such claims.

In the first place, it is essential to make a sharp distinction between effects within target areas and effects outside. There are four direct causes of death in a nuclear attack. (1) *Prompt gamma radiation.* A 10-megaton bomb would deliver lethal radiation over a radius of about two miles from the point of impact. (2) *Blast damage.* The blast of a 10-megaton bomb would shatter brick buildings within a radius of about seven miles and fling solid objects like paving stones and people around with the speed of bullets. (3) *Fire and suffocation.* A 10-megaton bomb could be expected to set nearly everything within a 25-mile radius on fire, and the resulting fire storm would kill people not only by incineration but also by suffocation, since it literally burns the oxygen in the air. (4) *Fallout.* This is the only cause of death in a nuclear attack that is reduced by shelters of the type usually considered. The fallout pattern depends upon weather conditions and the kind of weapon used, and hence is difficult to predict.

It is clear from these facts that family fallout shelters would not insure the lives of people who live, roughly, within a 25-mile radius of a target. To the contrary, such areas would become crematoria. Yet the main effort of the Civil Defense Program to date has been the marking and planned stockpiling of tunnels, subways, cellars, and the like *in mainly urban areas*. Given the short warning time in the case of surprise attack (perhaps 20 minutes or so), few people could even reach these locations, and those who did would most likely be burned, suffocated, or crushed in falling debris. A RAND study[6] estimates that in 10 to 15 years, and at an expense of some 150 billion dollars (three times our present defense budget), we could provide hard-rock "heavy" blast shelters for about 40 million people, "medium" blast shelters for 40 million more, and "light" fallout shelters for the remainder. A model hard-rock shelter for a whole city is provided by the geology of Manhattan Island; with 20 square feet per person (less than a 5×5 space) 800 feet below the surface, the four million or so inhabitants of the skyscraping city of New York could be packed into a buried citadel for as long as 90 days at an expense of about 600 dollars per person. This is the only way to save people (temporarily, at least) in major cities if they are nuclear targets.

It is also clear that the effectiveness of our Civil Defense Program depends heavily upon Soviet strategy. Blast shelters adequate for 10-megaton bombs could be completely useless for 20-megaton bombs. A 50-megaton weapon deliberately burst at high altitude could create a fire storm over an area as large as the state of Rhode Island. The distribution of attack in terms of tactical (our retaliatory missile sites and nuclear production centers) *vs.* strategic (civilian population centers) targets would also be a major factor influencing the effectiveness of any civilian defense system. In this connection, it should be noted that whereas it would take an estimated 300 megatons to knock out the hardened Titan missile sites around Tucson, Arizona, it would only take a single 20-megaton bomb to obliterate a soft target like the city of Chicago and its whole metropolitan area.

To the extent that sheltering civilian populations destroys the credibility of an opponent's first strike, and hence his use of nuclear blackmail, he might be expected to increase the size and

---

[6] R-322-RC. Original not seen. See Gerald Piel, "On the Feasibility of Peace," *Science*, 1962, *135*, 648-652.

change the type of his weapons so as to counteract this disadvantage. A partial shelter program could thus accelerate the arms race, which in turn would accelerate the shelter race—and both sides would find themselves digging deeper and deeper into the earth.

Much less attention in this debate has been paid to social and psychological effects, but they are at least as important, particularly as far as preserving our way of life is concerned.[7] To develop anything more than a token civilian defense system would require a degree of regimentation of our society unheard of even in wartime and fully matching what we call the "anthill" social structure of the Communists. It is well known that you cannot train people effectively by having them read books. Americans would have to drill repeatedly, and under adverse conditions (such as a stormy winter night). Extensive cadres of civil defense militia would be required to enforce complete obedience. People who panic and block community shelter entrances, people who forget to bring what they should or try to bring too much, and people who stand up on their feet and say the whole business is nonsense could not be tolerated. It is interesting to note in passing that already some New York high school students who refused to participate in shelter drills have been refused recommendations to college. In other words, effective civilian defense against full-scale nuclear attack would demand a degree of conformity that is completely incompatible with our democratic values.

What about the social and psychological aspects of shelter use in case of attack? Some of the more militant vigilantes in the suburban areas surrounding Los Angeles have already made plans to prevent the panic-driven mobs of this city from invading their communities—by force. Religious leaders have already become embroiled in controversy over the moral issue of gunning down one's neighbor if he tries to get into your shelter. Could we expect husbands not to try to find their families, mothers not to try to find their children, and stay for several weeks in a com-

---

[7] An excellent summary of these factors can be found in Arthur Waskow, *The Shelter-centered Society,* 1962, report of a conference sponsored by the Peace Research Institute.

munity shelter, when all communication has been disrupted and no one knows what has happened to anyone else? Even supposing that the whole family unit gets safely tucked into its backyard fallout shelter, could they stay in this cramped situation for many days without suffering unbearable conflict and stress? What about human curiosity? Could we expect people to perform faithfully all the necessary precautions for survival—against an *invisible* source of danger—when they are eager for release and curious about what has happened outside? True, a group of young military men "survived" two weeks in a cramped shelter, but they were well trained and knew there had been no real attack.

And what about survival in the post-attack environment? The naive picture usually presented shows a single, concentrated attack followed by two weeks of hiding, whereupon we all march proudly out into the brave new world—to begin preparing for the next war? The fact of the matter is that neither side will be capable of concentrating its missile attack into one overwhelming salvo for a long time, even if it were to choose this strategy. The more likely situation is intermittent bombing spread over a prolonged period. How will people plant crops in contaminated soil? They have been given "expert" advice to send one expendable man out in a tractor to scrape off the topsoil! How will they get medicines, ingredients for cooking, materials for clothing in a world where the whole system of transportation is paralyzed? How will they even cook their meals or keep themselves warm in houses completely dependent upon electricity, gas, or oil, when these utilities are not available? I would predict that many of the lives saved by sheltering would be lost in the months and years following all-out attack.

Finally, and I think most importantly, we must inquire into the effect of a civilian defense program upon the likelihood of nuclear war. Even with a shelter program of any conceivable magnitude, no one denies that all-out nuclear war would be the greatest catastrophe that has ever struck this nation. Therefore the only rational defense against it is to prevent its occurrence. The persuasive "insurance" analogy is entirely misleading. To be sure, buying automobile insurance does not make you more reckless on the highways, but neither does it influence the behavior of other drivers. Shelter-building does influence our opponent. Can we be so naive as to suppose that a full-scale civil defense program on our part would *not* induce the Soviets to do the same thing? The claims of another RAND report[8] that the Russians have already undertaken a substantial civilian defense program are belied by the failure of foreign correspondents and other travelers in that country to find anything remotely resembling such preparations. So far the Soviet operation seems to be mainly a pamphlet affair much like our own.

Before the Holifield Subcommittee holding hearings on civilian defense, Herman Kahn has argued that Soviet strategists would aim their first-strike missiles at our tactical targets rather than strategic targets like cities, because only in this way could they hope to minimize our retaliation. Therefore, the reasoning goes, a large-scale fallout shelter program for civilians makes sense. But we have already seen that it is much cheaper in terms of megatons expended to destroy "soft" cities than "hard" missile sites. Furthermore, as we continue to harden our land sites and make our Polaris submarines more elusive, we offer the opponent little choice but to strike at cities if he strikes at all. Yet, as we have seen, it is the densely packed cities that are most vulnerable to blast, fire, and radiation. And even if he did not deliberately aim at our cities in a first strike, the opponent certainly would do so in a second salvo or in retaliation against a first strike on our part.

What would be the most probable impact of an all-out civil defense program upon Soviet decision-makers? Herman Kahn[9] has stated what the effect of a Soviet defense program would probably be on us: "Non-military defense might strengthen the resolve of Soviet leaders and make it more difficult to deter them. . . . In particular, it could make a [Soviet] first strike appear more attractive." Simply substitute "American" for "Soviet" above and you have a good prediction of the Soviet reaction to us under similar conditions. According to Singer,[10] the Soviets might well

---

[8] By Leon Goure. RAND, 1960.

[9] R-322-RC. See Marshall Windmiller, "The Dangerous Fraud of Civil Defense, *Union Review*, 1960, *1*, 5-22.

[10] J. David Singer, "Deterrence and Shelters," *Bulletin of the Atomic Scientists*, 1961, *17*, 310-315.

assume that we were preparing either a preventive first strike or a pre-emptive first strike (afraid that they were about to attack us), and in either case would become much more liable to opt the opening first strike themselves.

What would be the most probable effects upon ourselves? It is true that the shelter issue has penetrated the screen of denial and has stirred up healthy debate. The fact that the public has refused to be stampeded into a helter-skelter shelter program is testimony to the essential good sense of our people when they become concerned, rather than their apathy, and it is an effective answer to those who believe the public should be kept in the dark about policy matters until the professional elite has determined the "correct" course.

But what if our people are finally frightened into committing their energy, time, and money to a massive civilian defense program? Several predictions can be made. First, having committed themselves, they will begin to rationalize and justify this behavior. As the investment increases, the program will gain momentum, and more and more fantastic underground structures will be demanded. People will become more easily angered by those who persist in denying the value of the program. The fury created by the frustrations of the program itself will be easily diverted onto The Enemy as the real source of all this disturbance and annoyance, and such fury will make it difficult for the government to negotiate effectively. Since civilian defense emphasizes the inevitability of war, we could expect lessened pressure on government to find better solutions. And since to commit themselves wholeheartedly to digging holes in the ground people must really have faith that it protects them, their resistance to risk-taking by military or political strategists would be weakened.

The present Administration has gotten itself into a corner on civilian defense, and I suspect it wishes it had never opened the Pandora's box it found there. Even if it could be demonstrated that the protection offered by fallout shelters more than balances the increased probability of nuclear war, a government cannot tell the half of the people who live in potential target areas that they are expendable. This is political dynamite. To protect *these* people we must either dig them deep into solid rock (which is both very expensive and very inhuman), or evacuate them from their cities (which is simply not feasible, unless done so far in advance that it becomes a threatening signal to the opponent), or . . . what?

There is another possibility here: we can make it less likely that people in cities will be targets for nuclear bombs. In the long run, this means gradually reducing world tensions and arriving at some form of international control—which is precisely the goal toward which this book is aimed. But we can also do something to help these people immediately. We can announce to the world that we are beginning to move all our missile sites and nuclear production facilities away from population centers and into remote and sparsely populated areas; we can invite the Soviets to reciprocate in kind, explaining that we no more desire to exterminate Russians than we want them to exterminate Americans; and then, as nuclear displacement is accomplished in area after area, we can invite the Soviets to inspect what is *not* there, and ask them to respond in kind. This application of GRIT would be mutually advantageous—and more. The clean geographical distinction between strategic and tactical targets would strengthen the moral distinction, would reduce tensions generally, and would therefore serve to stabilize the whole military situation in a meaningful way.

This consideration of the pros and cons of civilian defense in a nuclear age has been a long and rather grisly business, but it is an essential part of the Great Debate. I would conclude as follows. First, accepting the premise that the only real defense against nuclear attack is to prevent it from happening, I believe that an extensive shelter program would increase the chances of war out of all proportion to the number of lives it would save should such a war occur. Second, a civilian defense program does nothing to solve the problems that create wars in our time; to the contrary, it foreshadows a world of underground fortress states whose only likely interaction *would* be war. Third, even though individual citizens may see it as a defensive measure, in the strategic sense a massive shelter program is an aggressive step in the arms race, one which threatens the opponent into doing the same thing as well as into further increasing his offensive power. And last, humans being what they are, I am afraid that a civilian defense program with all the negative effects above still would offer little more than an illusion of security without its substance. Many who thought they were safe would just die, if not in the attack then in the grim months and years that would follow.

Which way, Homo Sapiens—back to the caves or out to the stars? Soon after our kind of primate came down from the trees, began to walk about on his hind legs, and realized he had a reversible thumb—soon, that is, as geological time is counted—he discovered that he was in an extremely unfriendly world and fled into the caves for shelter. Not too long after that, again as geological time goes, he was out in the open again but now armed with weapons of bone and stone, with fire, with language, and with the rudiments of social organization—and other things his big brain had devised. In an incredibly short time, on the same scale, man has conquered the earth. Other animals either serve or fear him. He has pried many secrets from Nature, and now even She, but for occasional rebellion, does his bidding. The only thing he has not been really able to understand and successfully control is himself.

His science and technology, his population, and his weapons are all increasing on positively accelerated curves. He can use the first to control the second. He can certainly reach the other planets of his own system and, perhaps with new scientific discoveries, the planets of other star systems. Many of these planets must be capable of supporting life. If he fails to control the spiral in armaments, then, of course, the population explosion may be damped quite abruptly, along with his accelerating science. We are living in an exciting period of human history. But it is also a very dangerous and threatening period. Will fear again drive us back into the caves, caves of our own devising and from which we may never return? Or will we stand free and clear in the open, using our big brains to solve this problem as we have others, with our eyes fixed on the stars?

The Task Ahead

Bringing the nuclear age under control is the biggest problem we have ever faced, and I have no illusions about my own capacity to comprehend it all. The problem does have psychological components—perhaps magnified in importance because they are so little understood—but much more than psychology is involved.

Political science, economics, anthropology, international law, communications, nuclear and space technology, and diplomacy, to name only part of the roll, all have pieces to contribute to the final solution. And no one as aware as I am of the strength of the contrary forces, of the momentum the arms race has built up, and of the deeply ingrained mechanisms of cold war thinking which drive the whole process could be very hopeful about our chances of escaping from this situation unscathed.

Nevertheless, I have convinced myself, at least, that it can be done. The policy of graduated and reciprocated initiative in tension-reduction that I have outlined is not an easy way out, and it may well contain flaws that I have not even considered. Yet it does seem to offer a possible course in which we could both maintain our security and begin moving toward a safer, more peaceful world. It is a policy designed to release us from the present freeze on initiative in foreign policy and the impasse in negotiations. As such, I think it merits serious consideration and evaluation.

True, it would require considerable understanding, trust, and self-restraint on both sides, but fortunately the policy includes mechanisms for developing such understanding, such trust, and such self-restraint in course. The hopeful side of the picture is the remarkable adaptability of the human species. The democratic system, too, is adaptable; it includes mechanisms for the discovery of fresh ways of solving social problems—if they are allowed to operate.

I hope I have convinced the reader as well. If so, the question uppermost in his mind at the moment undoubtedly is, "What can *I* do?" There is no simple answer to this question. Effective action springs from more than felt concern or felt efficacy; it takes the combination of both. Given a modicum of intelligence and the elimination of emotional denial, concern is readily generated. But how one can be most effective depends upon who he is, what role he plays in our society, what his particular talents are. Some people can be very effective carrying placards around the White House or the Russian Embassy; others can engage effectively in spirited public debate; others do much better behind a typewriter.

The media man. Here is a taboo question: just how free is our free press? The performance criterion is *diversity*. The less of it, whether due to government regulation or sheer conformity, the less freedom. Diversity is easy in things that do not count; it becomes difficult when issues of national concern are involved. If we agree that novel situations demand novel solutions, and that in a democratic society the mass media largely determine whether ideas can gain a hearing, then one critical role of the media in the development of policy becomes clear: enlivening the Great Debate. Have the mass media lost their traditional role of being the "watchdog on government" and assumed the more passive role of "engineering consent"? I realize that it is hard to buck the system—dependence on leased wire services, subservience to publishers, and printing what the public wants (or perhaps is believed to want)—but to accept these restrictions without a fight is to sacrifice the professional code.

There are also self-imposed restrictions on the freedom of our press. Media men are human, too. They are only *less* susceptible than the general public to the mental dynamics of the cold war, not immune to them. They, too, are prone to view the world in absolute blacks and whites and to interpret news events so as to preserve this oversimplified view. They are also prone to apply a double standard of national morality, to accuse the opponent of being evil in intent when he does what we also do for noble motives. They see conflict as more newsworthy than cooperation and conciliation—even though the latter are certainly more novel in our troubled world. It is crucial that we understand ourselves if we are going to have any hope of understanding others and find a way out of our dilemma. By understanding the mechanisms of cold war thinking, by being aware of the beam in our own eye, media people are best able to apply the necessary correction to the spectacles through which Americans see their world.

The housewife. Many women these days are asking themselves why they are planning so hard for the future—providing a good home, insuring that their families have healthy bodies and alert minds, saving money for college or for retirement—when the future could be taken completely out of their hands by forces beyond their community and, apparently, beyond their control. In rapidly increasing numbers they have been joining organizations like Women for Peace. I am told that the League of Women

Voters has made foreign policy one of its prime issues at the national level. Participation in such groups keeps one informed about basic policy issues that seriously affect our lives even though they seem remote; participation also provides an avenue for effective action.

There are many other ways the individual homemaker can have impact. She can hold "letter-writing coffee hours" at which a group of neighbors decide on the critical points to be made on some particular issue, but then go home and write their own, personal letters to congressmen, senators, or even the White House. Thoughtful personal letters *are* read and nearly always responded to. She can try to reach various community organizations, like the PTA and her church discussion groups, involve them in the issue of survival in a nuclear age, help them locate lecturers and discussion leaders, and keep them alerted to critical issues on the horizon. If her family were willing, she could offer to bring a foreign child to her home for a year of American living and schooling. When individual actions like these are multiplied by the hundreds of thousands, we discover that a great human force is being applied to policy decisions.

The congressman. I am sure that many times each year in the privacy of their own offices congressmen ask themselves this cruel question: how can I best serve the interests of my country, as well as my own constituents in the long run, and still get reelected? Inadequately staffed for all the jobs that must be done, for all the bills that must be read and understood, for all the hearings that ought to be attended, and under pressure from innumerable special interest groups, the congressman nevertheless tries to keep his head above the political waters. And it is hard to keep principles above politics; one can always rationalize that if he is going to do any real good for the country (tomorrow), he must stay in office.

Let me coin an epigram: *the more people who have integrity, the less it is needed.* Take the matter of Communist China. Almost everyone I have talked to has privately conceded that our failure to recognize the government of this giant nation and support its admission to the United Nations is sheer madness, yet how many have stood up and said so? In January, 1962, the House of Representatives passed H.R. 7927, a postal revenue bill carrying an amendment designed to prohibit the handling of Communist propaganda but so broadly worded as to shut off completely scientific, cultural, and other information from Communist countries. This bill passed the House by a vote of 127 to 2. How many congressmen who really opposed this oppressive legislation conveniently failed to show up and be counted? How many voted "aye" because they were afraid of being accused of being pro-Communist? If this amendment had been singled out, sharply criticized, and resoundly defeated 227 to 102, I am sure no one but Mr. Welch would have accused 227 congressmen of being soft on Communism.

The teacher. If there is any profession that is future-oriented, it is the teaching profession. As successive classes of bright young minds pass through the capable hands of the high school or college teacher, he must often wonder how they are going to end up. What kind of a world will these youngsters face when they are preparing another generation for his older, but perhaps wiser and gentler, hands? And there is probably no other profession that has easier access to the facts about our world and its problems, or is better equipped and trained to disseminate this information. The teacher is in an ideal position to further the Great Debate. And so are the minister, priest, and rabbi—who are also teachers.

One of the things that really puzzles me is why most intellectuals, equipped and trained as they are, have tried so hard to keep their brilliant heads in the sand. Of course, it is always easier to keep on doing what one has been doing—chalking the same old formulas on the board, doing the next experiment, writing another scholarly bit on the hair styles of the Egyptians in 4000 B.C.—than to launch oneself into an orbit from which there might be no return. But when he thinks about it, surely the teacher must realize that unless the problem of survival in a nuclear age is solved, and that pretty soon, children will not be around to copy down his formulas and our society will not be the kind that supports such frills as treatises on Egyptian hair styles. And more than this, I believe that intellectuals in our kind of society have more than a right to speak out—they have an obligation to do so. In a very real sense, our society has set them aside and invested much time and effort in their training deliberately, so that they can provide the cutting edge in solving society's problems. Yet the Association of American University Professors has maintained a most dignified and scholarly detachment as far as this issue is concerned.

The businessman. It is hard for a man to tend to his own business and at the same time to be a man of affairs. Faced with a bewildering array of first threats and then assurances from so-called "experts," the easiest solution seems to be to go on about business as usual and let the people up there in Washington worry about it. There are magnificent exceptions to this rule. I am thinking of the president of a corporation whose primary business is making electronic parts for missiles and space vehicles, yet who has been consistently and most effectively working for peaceful solutions. There are increasing numbers of organizations among businessmen—in advertising and in oil, as well as in defense industries per se—that have taken it upon themselves to become informed about policy problems and exert their influence.

There is also much that can be done at the community level. A well-informed local businessman can serve as the spokesman for concerned groups in his town or city. He is in a position to make contacts with opinion leaders, both within his own community and well beyond it. He is in a particularly good position to work with labor leaders and academic people on the complex problem of the economics of disarmament and how to plan intelligently for it. He can campaign for funds to bring outside speakers to his community to give public lectures on policy issues. And, of course, he can and should influence the decisions of local and national government through honest, unselfish lobbying. The purpose of all this is not to tell people *how* to think on these crucial issues, but rather to pull their heads out of the sand and make sure that they *do* think. If disaster does come, it may be easy to blame the egg-heads, the fools in Washington, or the devils in the Kremlin—but this will not help us.

It sometimes proves helpful to back off from a problem and try to view it within a larger chunk of space and time. Taking the long view in space, as from a planetary system many light-years away, the events that today are shaking the very fabric of our lives are all transpiring on the knife-thin edge of a little pebble in the sky, and they will not cause the slightest disturbance in the cosmos. Taking the long view through time, one can envisage the interlacing, ever-expanding tree of human life, bearing its generations of ephemeral blooms, yet but little affected by the changing national climates in its course. The organizations among men we call "nations" come and go—a name may persist and the human content change, or the reverse—and this is as true for what we now call "the Soviet Union" and "the United States" as it was for Rome and Babylon.

Viewed in sufficiently wide perspective, the crises we now face are only minor themes in the tapestry of the universe. But they are important to the individual human threads. As far as this particular little planet is concerned, we are now almost to the point where we can literally blow it apart. This, certainly, we do not want to do. And even though we may be willing to admit that nothing made by man will last forever, we nevertheless are rightly proud of our way of life in which individual human beings have dignity and freedom from oppression by their government. We want this way of life to endure, no matter what may be its name or who may be its champion.

The real question, I suppose, is whether the human species, like the dinosaur and the dodo before him, has arrived at the point where his own peculiar specialization has rendered him unfit for continued survival. We are, in truth, clever little fellows running around this globe with awesome devices in our hands, but directed by minds that often run in primitive channels. Is this our Achilles heel? With his giant foresight, Albert Einstein many years ago put it in words that might well have been written today: "Our world is threatened by a crisis whose extent seems to escape those within whose power it is to make major decisions for good or evil. The unleashed power of the atom has changed everything except our ways of thinking. Thus we are drifting toward a catastrophe beyond comparison. We shall require a substantially new manner of thinking if mankind is to survive."

And what is this *new manner of thinking?* It is not really new at all. Centuries before the nuclear age, Jesus Christ, in his role as a great social teacher, offered mankind the essence of the answer, both in how he lived his own life and in what he preached: Do unto others as you would have them do unto you. The example has been before us for 2,000 years. The time for putting it into practice is running out.